ENTERING THE

CORPORATE WORLD

A Fable with Powerful Secrets

By Stephen McLoughlin

TABLE OF CONTENTS

FIND THE PORTAL

So you want to make it in Corporate

America? Of course you do! Modern capitalism

allows the worker to convert the random anguish

and suffering of poverty into the structured

anguish and suffering of being a wage-slave. Who

would not want to gain a bit of control over the

maelstrom that we know as life? But how is it

done? How does one get in that door and sign-up

for a life of soul-shrinking drudgery, political

scheming, and paranoid obsessiveness? I know, it

seems mysterious and even unfair to the uninitiated. Here are these uninspiring college graduates dropping off the conveyor belts of colleges and universities, right into the warm corporate lap. You scowl and call out to a roommate, "Hey, that idiot, Roscoe Smith, that we had Accounting 101 with is now working at Big Global X and probably pulling down a massive salary … that guy couldn't answer one question from the professor for the entire semester. Remember?"

Your roommate laughs scornfully, "I know, I still remember his stock answer – the one he used when he was hungover and could not remember his name… 'Uh … I'll have to get back to you on that one … that's a tricky one.' It did not matter if the question was, 'Did you read chapter 4?' – That was still his answer." You nod enthusiastically,

feeling some illusion that you are successfully,
'Trying this rascal in the Court of Fairness.'

"Yes! I forgot about 'The Answer!' I still remember Professor Johnson frowning and looking at Smith as if he were an alien being who materialized only seconds before. Johnson even tilted his head to one side, like a dog hearing a high-pitched whistle. He was too civilized to take it any further though – he should have kicked Smith out of the class."

Roommate says, gloomily, "Yes, but there he is, making big money and probably driving an awesome car, and wearing his corporate badge even after hours, 'by accident' of course." You both grow silent, realizing once again that **there is no such place as,** *"The Court of Fairness."*

So how does it happen? You and your roommate have applied for work at hundreds of places; carried resumes in portfolios while you sweated in lobbies in your navy blue suits. You have been obsequious to everyone in your interviews, smiling and laughing like carefree children when that seemed to be the interviewers' intent, growing serious and frowning when the interviewer seemed to be mentioning something that required seriousness. Yet, you are not allowed in the sanctuary ... why not? *Why not you?*

Alternatively, you have finally entered the coveted portal, but you seem to be relegated to some anteroom, never invited to the important meetings; never promoted. You feel the breeze as people rocket past you on their way up the corporate ladder, while you clutch at it with sweaty palms, just hoping you won't fall. (Don't look down).

Rather than burden you with a load of boring business advice, I am going to convey all the business wisdom you will ever need, cleverly packaged in a short story – the story of Mr. Jones.

STEPHEN MCLOUGHLIN

Book 1: Entering the Corporate World   6

NURSE ANDROID

Jones woke up in a bed in a white room
that he had never seen before; it looked like a
hospital room. The room was well-lit, but there was
no sign of an overhead light or a lamp. There were
no windows. Once he sat up, an android nurse
glided toward him from a corner and greeted him
in a well-modulated voice. "Mister Jones! How nice
it is to see you conscious! I am Nurse Nancy. Is
there anything I can get for you? Perhaps you
would like a stimulant to start your day?"

Jones squinted at the android in annoyance, particularly offended by the fact that it looked just

like a beautiful woman dressed in a white uniform, except for the word "DROID" stenciled on its forehead and the fact that it rolled toward him with wheels on the bottom of its feet. The other clue was the fact that the nurse did not seem to be reading his reactions, but he did not care much about that. He wondered why anyone would deface an otherwise perfect replica of a person.

"You are staring at my forehead Mister Jones, with an expression of distaste, perhaps with a dash of confusion. Do you have a question?" Jones thought, *there goes my theory about not reading reactions...*

"No, no ... well yes, I do..." he stammered, blushing for no good reason. "Why do you have "DROID" stamped on your forehead? Did you lose a bet? Haha..." His laughter trailed-off lamely and he wondered why in the world he attempted to make a joke.

Nurse Nancy shrugged and smiled and said, "This is a legal requirement for all artificial life forms. A decade or so ago, there was a great outcry about the ethics of passing us off as real humans and the problems that could result from such things. The first requirement was that we all had to bear a clear stamp of what we are. This calmed some of the fear, but the 'wheels requirement' was added a few years later, to make sure that, even if we wore a hat or otherwise covered our "tattoo," we were still unmistakably a bucket of bolts."

Jones frowned at this, sensing the injustice and bitterness underneath the self-deprecating humor. He wanted to dig deeper, but decided he should find out where he was and why he was here. Jones asked, "Where am I? Am I prisoner? What do you want with me? How did I get here? Is this an experiment? Have I been given drugs? Are you going to kill me? Am I dreaming? If this 'android law' stuff happened a decade ago, why don't I remember it?"

Jones expected Nurse Nancy to tell him to slow down, to calm himself, that all questions would be answered in due time, etcetera, but she answered him without hesitation, which he decided made sense, given that she was not human.

"You are in a historical research facility. Yes, your movement is restricted, if you call that a 'prisoner.' We have some questions for you and then will return you to your time and place. You were brought here in a Time-Shifter by Doctor

Moran and her team. This is not an experiment, though Doctor Moran always learns something new from each session. Yes, you have been given drugs to facilitate the time-shift and your re-entry. There are no lasting ill-effects. No, we are not going to kill you – why would we? No, you are not in a dream-state. You do not remember the 'android law stuff' that happened a decade ago because it was a decade ago *for me*, but three hundred years in the future *for you*. Welcome to the 24th century Mister Jones."

Jones pondered all the answers for about 30 seconds and then asked to see Doctor Moran. Nurse Nancy beamed at him and applauded briefly. She said, "Excellent! An adventurer! Some people curl-up in a ball and cry when they are faced with so much change and uncertainty, but you are ready to get on with it! I love it!" Jones thought that if Nurse Nancy did not have those wheels and that tattoo on her forehead, he could really go for her. Come to think of it, he could probably get past his discomfort with the tattoo, and maybe the wheels were not really such a big deal...

Nurse Nancy pressed a button on something on her wrist and then went back to gliding around the room, checking gauges and tapping lit squares. "Doctor Moran will be here in 48 seconds, assuming the current pace of walking is sustained."

Doctor Moran bustled in, looking like the stereotypical physician /psychologist hybrid from the 21st century. White lab coat, spectacles, thinning hair, pale complexion, slight stoop, mild but thoughtful expression, abstract, distracted, socially awkward. He greeted Jones in a friendly manner, checked his pulse, listened to his heartbeat with a stethoscope, put that back in his lab coat pocket, nodded to Nurse Nancy, scribbled a note on a chart and put it back in a rack at the end of Jones' bed. Jones realized that he had not noticed the rack or the chart before.

"Excellent Mister Jones, excellent!" said Doctor Moran, nodding and smiling. "You came through in tip-top shape! You are wondering why you are here, how you came to be here and so on... I know. We are in the 24th century. We pull people into our time when we have a question for them, interview them, and then send them back. Sometimes we keep them, if they are needed over a long period."

Moran peered at Jones to see how we was taking all this news and seemed satisfied, so he continued, "Please follow me to my study; we will have a bit of lunch and then I can tell you much more about our world and perhaps ask you some questions as well." Moran chuckled drily, as if he was accustomed at be the only one who laughed at what he said.

Jones wondered whether all this was real and whether he should resist. He decided "no" to both questions and followed Doctor Moran out of the room, casting a last look at Nurse Nancy and giving her his best mischievous smile. She winked at him. He was completely fine with the wheels and tattoo at this point. They walked down a white corridor and Doctor Moran opened a wooden door labelled "Moran" and gestured for Jones to precede him into the room.

Jones entered the room and sat down on a small leather-like sofa. The room was spacious enough to hold the office furniture and the sofa, as well as a small table and a potted tree. There was a window on one side and the sun was shining into the office. It was, overall, a pleasant setting. Moran sat in a typical office chair of the 21st century, the kind with adjustable arms and a swivel base.

Nurse Nancy knocked briefly and entered with a tray of sandwiches and coffee and placed it on a table near Jones. Jones felt famished and began eating a sandwich of ham, cheese, lettuce and tomato, very fresh and very tasty. He turned to Moran and said, "Delicious! I would have thought that I would be eating little cubes of green and yellow mush and you would have to tell me what was, 'ham' and what was 'cheese.' Even the coffee smells like real coffee, not some kind of brown nuclear-waste-flavored swill. Amazing!"

Moran smiled indulgently and said, "It is not as miraculous as it may seem. Everything you are experiencing right now, my appearance, the

hospital appearance, the food, the coffee …
everything – is supplied by you. We have the
technology to reflect what you expect."

Doctor Moran smiled even more broadly
and said, "So you see, you did not really 'expect'
cubes of non-descript food and nuclear-waste swill,
or you would have received exactly that." Moran
even began to chuckle at this point, finding a depth
of amusement in this that Jones did not feel. "I'm
kidding; we sort of give you a nudge in the right
direction, with some 'hints' on top of the core
infrastructure."

Jones asked, "So what do you actually look
like then? Are you some giant worm sitting in a vat
of liquid protein, examining my tiny and pathetic
body on a plate?"

Moran instantly became serious and even
looked concerned, raising his hands and patting the

air, saying, "No, no, nothing so grotesque. I am a human being and you are in a research building – it's just that my clothing and general appearance are supplied by you. We no longer have to dress and groom in our world, we just apply our assumption filters and go on our way. My core infrastructure is not a *male* human, but it is *human*. When you heard, 'Doctor Moran,' you pictured what you see before you."

Jones pondered that for a moment and realized that Doctor Moran was telling him that she was a woman. Jones smiled and said, "So, I take it that you are telling me that you are a woman and that you are naked, under that filter."

Moran frowned, but continued, "As for the food, the core infrastructure is not some sort of 'slime' that you are imagining is real food – it is a basic food infrastructure that you have brought to the level of a ham and cheese sandwich through your assumptions. There is a big difference!"

Jones felt better and calmed down from the angry and paranoid state that was taking hold of him. He said, "Now that a few minutes have past, I still think the sandwich was pretty good, except the bread was a bit stale tasting. Everything else was great though!"

As was typical for Jones, the minute he was not in a panic, his mind returned to frivolous pursuits. "What about Nurse Nancy, what does she really look like? Does she have wheels on her feet, or did I assume that into existence? What about you? Are you then a naked woman, under the filters?"

Moran looked a bit annoyed and said, "Let's not worry about Nancy or my state of dress for the moment – we have many things to discuss.

Before I get to my questions, do you have questions about how we brought you to our time and what we want with you?" Jones said, "Sure - you know I do – so talk to me."

Moran sighed and looked down for a moment as if pondering something. She was wondering if the research team made a mistake in selecting Jones – he seemed like an idiot, or at least emotionally juvenile. How could he possibly have the answer to their questions? She looked at the book that contained the background information on Jones. She had read it carefully, but she had expected someone with more depth as she was reading it.

Jones looked at her and decided that he did not trust her. He tried to "expect" an open field with no walls, flowers everywhere, Nurse Nancy running around without wheels, and no more

Doctor Moran, but nothing changed. He told

Doctor Moran, "Be warned that I am a martial arts

expert. I can subdue you and even take your life

within a matter of seconds, using my bare hands. I

can then escape from this nuthouse and make my

way home. Do not attempt to detain me."

Doctor Moran thumbed through the book

and smirked. She looked up for a moment and said,

"It is true that you had a, 'Kung Fu period' when

you were thirteen. You acquired a few books on Ju-

jitsu, Karate, and Judo. You practiced for a few

weeks and then used it to beat-up your younger

brother and a neighbor child younger than you.

Your father confiscated your books so you could

'cool off' and, 'reflect on the true spirit of marital

arts.' " You never resumed your training. You are

hardly what I would consider 'dangerous' Mister

Jones."

Jones laughed and nodded for a few moments, and then said, "Good job. Excellent research! Now get on with your questions and then get me out of here. By the way, what happened to transportation and energy over the centuries? Is there something I can invest in or seem to 'invent' when I get back so I can at least *profit* from this nightmare?"

Moran seemed to want to help and was ready to answer any question. "By the end of your century, the energy problem had been solved. There was no further need for fossil fuel or even hydrogen, wind, or solar power. All those sources were made obsolete by an extremely simple discovery, really just an understanding, of principles that had always existed. It's a shame, really, you had basically solved the problem with the discovery of quantum physics, but you went for decades pounding on the same old methods."

"It was the same with 'Assumption Filters,' they are of incalculable value and people had intuited the basic principles by the time of Plato's Cave, yet nothing was done for centuries. In your time, people said, 'Perception is reality,' but took it not further. Can you imagine the drop in resource consumption from your time to ours? We do not consume even 1% of what you consumed in plastic, livestock, crops, metals, coal, oil, timber, and so on – you were destroying the world at breakneck speed. Most of that consumption was just to satisfy people's expectations. Think of that!"

Jones was losing interest already and began staring at the doctor's shoes, wondering why he would have assumed black wingtips with slight scuffing of the toes. Where did these assumptions come from? What about those 'hints' that she mentioned? Did she have some indications on top of her core infrastructure to intentionally toy with his assumptions?

He was still listening with half his attention, in case the doctor said something he could profit from when he returned home. Something did catch his ear at that point.

Moran was saying, "Energy was always there, in the dual-state of quantum matter. Particles in a quantum state have a potential energy that can be tapped as soon as the uncertainty of the duality is resolved. This can be repeated endlessly and provide energy forever at minimal cost. It was there all the time."

Moran must have noticed the gleam in the eye of Jones because she added, "First, I doubt that you understand what I am saying and, second, if you take such things back to your world, you will be institutionalized. Others have tried it before you, against my advice, and are now in mental hospitals."

Jones nodded absently, thinking that it might be difficult to explain what he is hearing right now, but if he could steal something from here and now and take it back to his time, then he could reverse-engineer the item, with some help, and be a billionaire.

Jones began to look around Moran's office for something he could hide in his pocket. Did he have a pocket? He checked, yes, he had big front cargo pockets on his white coveralls. Moran was laughing and watching him. Jones wondered, *"Now, what is her problem?"*

Moran said, "You are wondering what you can take from my office back to your world. No, we do not have the ability to read minds yet, but you are a bit obvious sometimes." Moran tossed Jones an ink pen and Jones caught it. Moran said, while trying not to laugh, "Take a look at that when you get home." Jones looked it over, noticed that it looks like one of his standard issue office pens.

Jones tossed the pen back to Moran and said, "I get it already – I'm not a complete fool, you know – the pen is supplied by my mind – there is no pen, so when I get home my pocket will be empty. In fact, I may not be wearing pants at all. Very clever...very amusing... Don't you sometimes need metal, or plastic, or cement, or something real? What about these 'core infrastructures?' Not everything can just be imagined. What do you do when you actually need something -- get your hands dirty and mine something from the ground?"

Moran shook her head, "Goodness no, we don't know how to *mine things* – we just take things from your time and bring them here. Your junkyards are an endless supply of steel, plastic, rubber, and so on, and you never miss the things we take. Why would we 'make' something? Ha! That's ridiculous. By the way, the pen would still be a pen when you returned to your time – in fact, it is *from* your time, but that's another story, for later."

Jones was getting really annoyed with Moran's superior attitude. "So you steal from us – that's what you call an advanced civilization?"

Moran did not lose her smile. "When you mined coal from the ground, you were borrowing trees from the past – didn't you know? When you extracted petroleum from the ground, you were going back in time to get zooplankton and algae subjected to immense heat and pressure. We, on the other hand, are taking your *garbage*."

"Okay, so you have everything figured out -
good for you, so why am I here? Can we get this
over with, so I can go home?"

DYSTOPIA

Moran realized that Jones was running out of patience and might act in some unpredictable manner if she did not get to the point of the visit and send him back home, so she became serious. "I am not a physician or a psychologist as you assumed. In our time, a person is not just one thing, as they were (or are) in your time. I am an investigator-historian-psychologist, specializing in the first half of the 21st century. It is a great pleasure to meet you and speak with you! I would like to ask you a few questions about some things that occurred, or are occurring, in your time, in your workplace. These events might be commonplace to you, but they are fascinating to us. We are actually writing a book about the workplace of your time." Jones remained silent, wondering how the concept of 'book' had survived.

Moran said, "The thing is, work in our time has become unnecessary for many people. People are bored and are beginning to play in other times, including yours. This is beginning to contaminate the history of your time and we are finding it necessary to remove some people from various times and to try to restore things to their original state, as much as possible. Our Directors think that we might have to recreate some sort of workplace from the past, just to keep people safe and give them something to do."

Jones felt the balance of power shifting a bit at this point. Moran seemed less confident and smug, while Jones began to wonder what he could get for a reward for his cooperation. He asked, "Can't you just block the use of time machines? Surely you have the technological skill to do that."

Moran shook her head, "No, actually, we cannot stop them. Personal time-shifters are ubiquitous now and to intervene with them, say with an electronic pulse broadcast, could easily kill people. We do not want to hurt people."

Jones was still confused and asked, "Why would anyone leave your utopia – doesn't everyone get what they want all the time? Isn't all competition for resources moot, so people can just have fun? Why would anyone want the soul-deadening totalitarianism of the workplace of the early 21st century?"

Moran nodded, and looked down, "One would think we would be happy as we are, but it has not been the case. There are people who find this world boring, they are sick of Assumption Filters and want to know what the core infrastructures are. They want to have things happen to them that they do not expect. They want unpredictability and what they call the 'creativity of the universe' in their lives."

Jones smiled, "What a mess! By the way, what is the 'core infrastructure' of Nurse Nancy - some big dude with a mustache? Why should I cooperate with you if you will not even answer my basic questions?"

Moran sighed and tapped some yellow dot on a panel over her desk. Jones smirked and looks at the ceiling. Nurse Nancy came into the room within a minute. Moran talked in a clipped tone,

"Nurse, I am going to turn off your assumption filter for a few seconds, at the special request of Jones. I know this is a violation of your privacy and I would like your express permission to do this. I apologize for the intrusion."

Nurse Nancy calmly said, "Doctor Moran, you have my express permission to disable my assumption filter for up to thirty seconds." Nancy handed a plastic square with illuminated dots to the doctor and stepped back two steps as if posing for a photograph. Moran studied the badge for a moment and then tapped the colorful dots in what seemed to be a pattern.

Jones stared fixedly at the nurse. He was surprised to find that she really was an android, with wheels and a tattoo on her forehead. Jones was baffled and said, "You mean the word 'droid' and the wheels are part of her core infrastructure? No way! Why would that be necessary?"

Moran started to speak and then hesitated and looked at Nurse Nancy. She thanked the doctor and left. As the door closed behind Nancy, Moran turned back to face Jones and said, "The government has, for a few years now, been supplementing the assumption filters in certain cases. They can do this on a mass scale, the filters designated by identifying codes that reveal their categories and sub-categories." Moran paused, noticing that Jones was frowning. "What?"

"Well, this is not very utopian, is it? This went from a happy little story about conservation of resources to a dystopian nightmare about thought control ... didn't it?"

Moran closed her eyes and shook her head wearily. "No, it did not become a 'dystopian nightmare' – there is a public good that can be realized by the very controlled, very selective, supplementation of certain filters – that's all. Yes, there is a brain-computer interface; of course there would have to be, but that does not mean there is thought control."

"Oh, yes it does." Jones said, "People are talking about brain-computer interfaces even in our time, as if it is the only way to make the next big steps of progress, but they don't know what they are getting into. The computer will be staring into our brain even as we are staring into the computers' – echoes of Nietzsche's warning… or maybe Orwell… this is like "1984," only the timing was off."

"Rubbish!" Moran angrily stood up and paced the area in front of her desk. "There is nothing in common with that novel! Our speech and thoughts are free. We are free to assemble and free to dissent. You have no idea how different we are from what you are implying!"

Jones took a deep breath and exhaled. "Ok, maybe it was slightly off the mark, but you really have no idea whether you are free to speak or assemble or dissent because you have no idea if what you perceive is true. You might *think* you are assembling with 200 like-minded activists to protest the supplementation of filters, when you are really assembling with 200 hamsters that are running around in circles looking for biscuits. You lost all freedom at the moment when you allowed any tampering with the filters – any at all."

Moran had nothing to say, but resumed her seat and just kept shaking her head, while avoiding eye contact with Jones.

Jones said, "I'm sorry, but you did – you lost your freedom. I don't know why they are called "assumption filters" either – that makes it sound as if they filter *out* assumptions, not filter them *in*. How is anyone going to learn anything or progress past their assumptions, if all they ever perceive are their assumptions?"

Moran pounced on this: "Exactly so! That was the justification for the supplementation of the filters when it was first proposed. The idea is that they work fine on the everyday level, but that there should be a gradual narrowing of the gap between people's assumptions and the reality of the matter."

Jones was not impressed. "Same old problem: who gets to decide what reality is? For example, you are a woman and I assumed you were a man because I am steeped in gender stereotypes from my epoch. Your government could decide to supplement my erroneous assumption and add that you are a woman, but I might also have the wrong race, wrong height, wrong everything – why not fix all of it … oops, that would be exactly what we started with since the dawn of existence – also known as 'reality'."

Moran was clearly exhausted with Jones and said, "That is a ridiculous oversimplification and full of sweeping generalizations. For the most part, the Assumption Filters work spectacularly well and save a massive amount of resources."

Jones decided that no one was going to win this argument, so he fell silent, pondering whether Nurse Nancy would come back to his time with him when he left – if he ever did – and whether he could get rid of some of the supplemental stuff that the government had added – no wonder she was bitter.

Jones asked, "On a different topic, what is this shyness about nudity? You blushed when I asked if you were naked. I would have thought that by this time, people would have outgrown such primitive taboos as nudity." Jones struck a superior pose at this point and dropped his head a bit just so he could peer upward at Moran.

Moran watched him thinking, *He is not an idiot, as much as a -- buffoon ... yes, I think 'buffoon' is a better word.* She said, "It's not a taboo, it is simply a sense of privacy that people have never 'outgrown' because it is a simple human instinct to cover certain parts of the body."

Jones said, "Okay, whatever – what is the native stuff that you wanted to ask me about? What are you trying to figure out? Do you want to know what it feels like to be in our time and suffer the angst and humiliation of having to cater to inflated egos, just to get currency to exchange for basic necessities? It is so much fun."

Moran said, "We want to know everything! It is such a puzzle, that is, the workplace of your time is so difficult for us to understand." Moran picked up a blue book from her desk and perused it for about a minute, then closed it and put it back on the desk. Jones noticed with some amusement that Moran could not leave the book as it was placed, but had to position it exactly square with the desk edge. *A bit compulsive are we?*

Moran finally spoke, "You have a colleague by the name of Greg Hamby. He came to your company about eight months ago and was employed as an analyst. He is considered very talented and is already discussing an opportunity with your manager for the position of Senior

Analyst." Moran stopped and leaned back a bit in her chair and watched Jones to see how he reacted.

Jones nodded periodically through the comments and then shrugged. "So?" Moran nodded, "So far, so boring, right? Now consider that Hamby is from *our* time, from my team actually, not your time and that he has infiltrated your time to study you. What do you think of that? Moran smiled and raised one eyebrow, "Still boring?"

Jones laughed, "*Hamby*? Hamby is an *alien*?" Jones saw Moran scowling and quickly corrected himself, "Not an alien, but I mean a time traveler from the 24th century? What is he doing, taking pens from our time and bringing them back for you guys to remember what one looks like?" He was raising his eyebrows and shaking his head and smiling, all of which seemed to annoy Moran even further.

"No, he is not 'stealing pens' - usually. I implore you to take this research seriously. Hamby is (or was) gathering information from your time that we could not get from history books. He has done this research at considerable personal risk. Imagine what could happen to him if he is discovered to be a time traveler."

Jones was suitably chastised by this rebuke and said, "Okay, okay, I will provide what information I have. Hamby has been a real pain to me by the way. Anyway, how do people time-travel though? You have talked plenty about assumption filters and you have somewhat explained your energy source, but none of that explains how you guys are going back and forth in time so easily."

Moran nodded, encouraged by Jones'
commitment to cooperate with her. "It's a fair
question. Once again, the answer turned-out to be
amazingly simple, something that was right under
your noses all along, you basically just had to
change your thinking, not to change the world."

Moran swiveled in her chair in excitement,
looking upward in search of the right words for
Jones. "The way that I understand it is, that time,
after all, is linear and unidirectional. The idea that
all of time is happening all at the same time and
one only has to skip through some membrane to
enter a different time is not correct. All things
decay, even the sun – it is not a circle, but a line ...
but I digress."

Moran stood up and walked to the window
and looked out for a moment, walked back to her
chair and sat down. "So, thus far it seems *more*

difficult than what people thought, not *less* so, but wait! Think about the uncertainty principle and what actually resolves it – an observation! I have already explained how we mine this principle for energy, but it can also transport anyone anywhere and anytime – not just, 'leaving anytime' but literally *going* to any time."

Jones said, "I hope the amazingly simple part is coming soon, because I don't feel it yet." Moran nodded quickly, absently, and said, "I know, I will speed it up. So, create an observation of a person, then reduce the person or object to its composite particles in a 'sealed container,' then store that collection of particles on what you would call a 'computer hard drive,' set the date at which you want to reconstitute those particles, and then 'recreate the observation' of those particles while still in the sealed container."

Moran was beaming at Jones as if she expected him to slap his forehead, exclaim, "How obvious!" and run from her office to build a time machine. Instead, Jones was squinting at her and finally said, "Right, just, 'set the date' then simply, 'create an observation' … how could we miss it?" He shook his head and sighed. "Let's just forget time-travel, go ahead and ask your questions."

Moran seemed momentarily deflated by this sarcasm, but rallied and said, "I am going to ask you to walk down the hall with me to meet Hamby and to hear what he has to say about certain events; the questions will make more sense after that."

MOEJOE

Jones agreed to go with Doctor Moran and she led down a corridor. Jones couldn't keep from wondering if it really was a corridor, or just a dirt path; if there were really walls or just trees. Were they, in fact, walking across a tightrope with a seething mass of poisonous snakes beneath them? ...And so on. He had not thought to ask Moran what would happen if one assumed that one was walking on a bridge, but really there was no bridge there – would one fall to one's death, or would the assumption filter keep the bridge in place all the way over the chasm? In other words, could assumption filters counteract gravity?

Just in case, he walked in a perfectly straight line, putting one foot exactly in front of the other. Moran was getting too far ahead and she stopped and looked back at him. Moran said, "You are not really 'cut out' for this century, are you?"

Jones decided that this was a rhetorical question and did not take his eyes from his path, but finally said, "Just trying to avoid the secret snake pit. Anyway, all the science fiction writers predicted that we would have anti-gravity gear by now and would not even be walking on the actual ground… where is that stuff?" Moran laughed and said, "Yes, I find the science fiction novels of your time very entertaining. The whole anti-gravity thing is ridiculous. Gravity is absolutely essential for human life and movement." Moran paused and allowed Jones to catch up to her, then continued, "The idea that people would be safe to fly around in a vertical position is ridiculous. Why do you think birds fly horizontally? That is to reduce drag and to present a minimum surface area to collide with things. It's just hilarious – it's like penguins zooming around while still standing."

When they reached the laboratory and Moran pushed through a swinging door, Jones dropped the 'single path' theory and walked normally again.

Doctor Moran was greeted by a man in a red clown wig, clown nose, clown make-up, red suspenders, a striped red-and-white shirt, blue pants and giant red shoes. Doctor Moran said, "MoeJoe, this is Jones, our witness for the investigation. Jones, this is 'MoeJoe the Clown' –

his choice of names - my senior researcher. You
know him as Greg Hamby." As they shook hands,
Jones thought about his difficult relationship with
Hamby; how he had grown to really dislike the
guy. Hamby seemed to be questioning and
contradicting everything he said.

Jones asked, "Am I just *assuming* that he
looks like a clown, because I am so far unimpressed
with your operation, or is he really a clown?" Jones
could not help but smirk as he asked the question.
It was as if he got to call this guy a 'clown' without
repercussion; even to call the operation 'clownish.'

To Jones' surprise, Moe winked at him and
said, "It's not just you – this is my supplemental."
Jones looked baffled and turned to Moran, who
appeared to be busy looking through an instrument
much like a 21st century lab microscope. Moe
whispered, "I hacked the supplemental, man, it's

possible after all." He cast a look at Doctor Moran
and said, "She pretends she doesn't know. She's a
great boss." Moran frowned into the microscope
and said, "MoeJoe, show Jones the artefacts."

Moe nodded and walked over to a wooden
box on a bench and opened the lid, peered inside
and started pulling things out of it and tossing
them onto the floor. There was a variety of office
supplies and decorations. Moe stopped,
straightened up, and turned to Jones. "Recognize
that stuff? That's straight off the desks and walls in
your department. You guys think people are
stealing from you. You've been blaming the
custodial staff for months."

Jones was a bit rattled by the appearance of
the artefacts. "So we 'think' people are stealing
from us and … what? They are actually *donating*
stuff to us? You _are_ stealing from us – you're just

not the custodians. How did you get this stuff – did you come to our time yourself?"

Moe was not discomfited by the question. He dropped into a chair with wheels and scooted backward toward his workbench. "Yep, I came there myself, disguised as a custodian, and just filled-up a bag with stuff. No wonder you guys are blaming the cleaning crew. Someone probably spotted me."

Jones walked over to the pile and nudged the composition book with his toe and asked, "So what? What are you guys so giddy about? You time-traveled back a few hundred years and all you got was *this* lousy stuff? I would have mailed you a box of this for a few bucks."

Moe smiled broadly and said, "It is not exactly as it appears. This is swag man! (I got that word from your time). I am going to turn off all the assumption filters in one shot with my, 'Disabler of Assumption Filter Functionality,' affectionately dubbed, 'DAFFY' in honor of that immortal duck." Moe grabbed something like a bazooka off his workbench, positioned it on his shoulder, aimed it at the pile of stuff and pulled the trigger. There was a 'boom' and, for a few moments, the pile was covered in a smoke cloud.

When the smoke cleared, Jones could see the core infrastructure of the items in the pile. Some were small squares of cardboard, some were rectangles of metal; some were just cheap, battered versions of the filtered items; all of them had at least some hint as to what they should be.

Moran asked, "MoeJoe, how much of that 'DAFFY' smoke and noise is necessary for the tool to work?" Moe smirked and said, "None of it" and turned back to Jones. "I brought all this stuff to your time and back here again. I was able to pass it off as manufactured in your time."

Jones could not fathom why anyone would want to come and "play" in the mindless drudgery of his office environment. He sat frowning and pondering, while Moran and Moe watched him closely. Finally, he asked, "Why did you come there? What do you want?"

Moe scooted over to where Moran was leaning against the work table and asked, "How much can I tell him?" Moran sighed, "As much as you want, he is going to eventually ask anyway, given what I have seen from him thus far." Moe said, "Fair enough" and kicked the table to zoom his chair back over to Jones.

"Brother Jones, I know that as 'Greg Hamby' I have been a real 'piece of work.' I seem charming and brilliant to your executives, but arrogant and self-centered to my colleagues. I even went back and forth in time so that I could be right about everything. That was very amusing, I can tell you. I have, in fact, duped even *you* a few times – sorry about that. Once, when you had a great idea and had the courage to propose it in a meeting with me and your management, I went back and forth in time and made sure that your idea would fail, just to help me get promoted."

Jones noticed that Moe could not refrain from laughing as he shared this little anecdote. Jones said, "You are not a very good person, are you, Moe?" Moe only smiled at Jones, noticing that Jones seemed to be very quick to anger.

Doctor Moran stood staring out of the window, appearing not to be paying attention, but she asked, "By the way, we also noticed that you snatched a 'Venti Latte' from Hamby's desk and tossed it in a restroom trashcan. I think it was the day after he spent the night with a woman you have been pursuing for months."

Jones frowned and shook his head, then appeared to remember and said, "Oh that! Yes, well you have drawn a causal link between two events that may have been close together in time, but have no cause-and-effect relationship. I merely noticed the coffee was too close to the edge of Hamby's desk and removed it as a safety hazard. Those big coffees can be dangerously hot!"

Moran and Moe looked at each other and laughed as if Jones were joking. Moran said, "I forget that people in your time actually tried to give *reasons* for behavior, as if it made any difference. By the middle of your century, the concept of "truth" had lost all meaning and thus all utility. People stopped differentiating between truth and lies. No one bothered making excuses anymore."

Moe added, "Research had firmly established that behavior was driven by a mix of instinct and the mindless repetition of behavior observed as a child. Why should anyone give "reasons" for their behavior?"

Jones said, "Ok, forget what I said – I took the coffee because I took the coffee. You also tried to give a reason, only you gave a different reason."

Moran said, "Yes, you had a reason, I am not saying that your action was a reflex. I am just saying that the reason was not the reason you offered and probably not a conscious reason at all. Anyway, by the 22nd century, all of a person's future behavior could be forecast, using predictive models. Some people opted-out of knowing what they were going to do, but many people studied their reports and tried, at first, to change their behavior. This caused great stress and unhappiness, so most people settled on reading the report, then setting it aside and living their lives. In our time, early interventions, both genetic and psychological, keep most people from any unhappy actions."

Jones rolled his eyes, "Here we go again, the weird little dystopian, controlling, police state, disguised as a progressive and free wonderland. I am beginning to understand why so-called 'criminals' like Hamby are coming to my time."

Jones began to look closely at Hamby/Moe and said, "So you also changed your filter to make yourself look handsome? That was not really fair for the rest of us guys. You are a bit of a weasel, aren't you?"

STEPHEN MCLOUGHLIN

Moran said, "Things are applicable to their time – they make sense in context. If you could describe the workplace of your day to a person from the 19th century, you would see similar reactions, or even more vehement ones. Really, imagine telling someone from the 19th century that someday people who sit 10 feet apart will be sending each other electronic mail to avoid human interaction. By the way, MoeJoe did not change his looks – he really is that handsome."

Moran continued, "Seriously though – you have so-called 'Managers' chastising and praising employees in these 'emails,' rather than speaking to them… it is really bizarre when viewed from our time. We saw a case in your world where a manager told someone to open the blinds on the window, via electronic mail, while sitting in the same office area. We had a good laugh over that one."

Moe added, "Not to mention what could happen if the subordinate resisted in any way. We had a guy illegally time-travel back to the 21st century and he was fired before we could even arrest him. His fault really … he should have studied the time before he jumped. Then he might have known not to express himself openly – it was pitiful, he just slunk back to our time and gave himself up."

Jones asked, "What did you do to him - chemically castrate him or 'remedially educate' him?"

Moe laughed and looked at Moran to answer. Moran said "Jones, you really have read too many dystopian novels; we don't act like your Stalinists or Maoists, I think he was asked to perform 6 months of community service, working at a center for the elderly."

Jones was surprised and said, "Elderly? I thought you would have solved the aging problem by now and, in fact, people would live to be 1,000 years old and look like 20-year-olds their whole lives. Not so, I guess."

Moran looked at Jones with some curiosity. "You know, at first glance, you seem like a rather low-intelligence specimen, but you are actually quite clever, in a sort of manipulative, tactical way."

Jones smirked, "You are the ones who no longer have a concept of truth – why am I the manipulative one? Did you not confess that you are a culture of amoral narcissists?"

Moran looked at Moe and he smiled at her. Moran turned back to Jones and said, "See? You keep slightly changing the subject to where you feel you can make a point. If you cannot think of anything to score on, you change the subject entirely. In no case do you ever admit fault or show any sort of humility or self-awareness."

Moran continued, "As I mentioned, MoeJoe and I are writing a book about your time. Please come back to my office with me and review it for us."

Moe slid off the chair and followed them. He was rather tall and seemed to have to lag and wander a bit to avoid walking ahead of everyone. When they reached the office, Moran and Jones returned to their previous seats and Moe went to perch on the window ledge.

Moran picked-up a paperback book from her desk and said, "We started by describing this odd concept of 'team' from your world. We decided that there are four identifiable types of teams. See what you think." She tossed the book to

Jones and he looked it over. It started off in an unpromising manner, with an introduction that compared the worker to a cockroach infected by a parasite. Jones wondered whether Moran and Moe really had any promise as writers.

THE COCKROACH WASP

The Emerald Cockroach Wasp temporarily paralyzes a cockroach and then injects its brain with neurotransmitters that make it submissive, though alive. The wasp lays its egg in the cockroach and the larva eats the roach as it matures, then bursts out of it. What does this have to do with working in the corporate world? It is exactly the same! Your manager wants you to be submissive and to allow him to grow and prosper at your expense. You have been injected with the neurotoxin of money and will passively watch as this happens. This is all fine, as far as it goes, but this book will guide you through that process of working within the constraints of an archaic, hierarchical system. Let us start by examining the 4 types of teams that you are likely to encounter in the workplace.

THE 4 TYPES OF TEAMS

"The Quilting Bee"

Everybody wants to get along. The team members constantly seek consensus. An angry word is never spoken. The only outputs are process-related; no actual work is done. Everyone goes in to the meeting quiet and morose, but comes out smiling and laughing and they can hardly wait for the next meeting. They can tell you at any time what "phase" the project is in, whether the status is "green light" or "yellow" – they would never allow it to "go red," and what the "ETA" is for the delivery date.

"The Angry Juror"

One person is the proverbial 'fly in the ointment' that keeps everyone from reaching consensus and going home. This person is seething with barely-contained rage and is prone to rant about things that can never be fixed. The angry one is entertaining for those on the team with a high tolerance for conflict. Sometimes there is some work done, depending on whether the angry dissenter can convince others to come aboard and vice-versa. People go into this meeting casting sidelong glances at the dissenter, afraid of direct eye contact, which could trigger a rant.

Moran and Moe looked at each other and Jones said, "No, that is not me." Moran only shrugged and smiled.

"The Process Masters"

This team makes a virtue of planning and organizing. Like the "Quilting Bee," they do not have

measurable output, but unlike the quilters, they may not
even like each other or have any fun; they are creating
structure "around" everything they can find. They offer
the structure and process to management as if it were a
deliverable. They put on a serious and even worried face
coming and going from the meeting – so much to do! No
matter how the project is going, their answer to a status
request will always be that there are, "some challenges"
and "some serious concerns."

Jones looked up for a moment and said, "Accurate so far, but I am not sure about the need to describe what their faces are like as they come and go from meetings."

Moran said, "It is terribly interesting for us and to our readers – so different from how we, in our time, act at work. People love the extra commentary, especially those who have not had the privilege to travel to your time for themselves."

"5 Jockeys on one Horse"

A team that finds the one industrious person –
someone who feels it necessary to produce actual work,
then rides that unfortunate soul to the finish line. The
other members of the team continually thank and praise
the workhorse, but do nothing to help them. These people
generally go into the meeting room laughing and come
out laughing – why not?

Jones laughed and said, "That's me! I am
the workhorse; everyone puts all the serious work
on me!" Moran and Moe looked at each other and
said, "The Angry Juror" simultaneously. Jones said,
"We will agree to disagree about my profile, but in
any case, I can tell you that this is good so far; you
just need a softer introduction, if your readers
expectations are anything like they are in my day."

"Moran said, "Of course, yes, we will go
back and work on that later. Right now, we want to

get our research on paper and check our

assumptions with someone who would know.

Please, read on, we next describe the types of

workers. I imagine that we are a bit off the mark on

some of those." Moran seemed friendly again,

more like she had at first, before all the back-and-

forth about Nurse Nancy, nudity, and 1984.

"Would you care for some coffee or any snacks

while you read?" Jones said, "No, I'm good. I'm

really not very high-maintenance, despite my sleek,

pampered, handsome appearance." Moran resisted

the impulse to scoff and only glanced at the book in

Jones' hand. Jones read aloud, "'The Six Types of

Worker...' Should be interesting..."

THE SIX TYPES OF WORKER

The Lifer

Not leaving, not advancing, hates everyone, but hides it most of the time, seethes with bitterness about the disappointments of life and the workplace. The Life can be easily spotted by the battered personal items around their work area, such as old coffee cups, outdated family photos, and greeting cards from years past. It is

easy to get along with the Lifer – just be sure you never
even appear to threaten their job security.

Jones said, "This is strong language – 'hates everyone.' Do you really want to say that without any empirical evidence to substantiate such a claim?"

Moe said, "I know, I never liked that sentence, but Doctor Moran was adamant that we keep it. I watched those people closely, even lived with some of them for a while. Some of them definitely did not have warm feelings for their coworkers, but the word 'hate' seems a bit strong." Moran said, "Okay then - take it out." Jones continued reading aloud.

The Neurotic

This may not be a true category, since most of
the other types are neurotics as well, but we decided to
keep it as its own type, since some workers are only

unique in that they demonstrate massive neuroses. This type usually has a high startle response, so be careful to make some warning noise as you approach them!

The Schemer

The Schemer actually loses sleep in the practice of plotting workplace machinations. The purpose of the scheming is ostensibly to strengthen job security or obtain advancement, but really the schemer schemes in order to feel some sense of control - all the reasons are 'a posteriori.'

The schemer noticed early in life that desires could sometimes be fulfilled through the manipulation of others and this gave him or her a sense of control over others. The control was a means to an end, i.e., getting what he or she wanted. Now, there may be no specific needs or even wants, except that sense of control – it has become an end in itself. The Schemer is difficult to get along with – just be careful about how you answer their questions and what you commit to writing – they

schemer may have dug a hole for you to fall in. They can

be safely handled only by considering them to be a live

explosive device that you must handle. No conversation

is trivial; no question is harmless; no request is without

a pitfall. If you can make them appear to win, they will

leave you alone for a while.

Jones laughed for a few moments after reading this one, and said, "Deep, very deep, guys."

The Baker

The Baker is sometimes also a Lifer, making life

a bit more bearable by ostensibly bringing cakes and

cookies for all to enjoy, but actually disguising the fact

he is eating ridiculous amounts of sugar to stay

motivated enough to put one foot in front of the other.

The Baker is happiest when he is complimented on the

baked goods he brings, while sampling a few items

himself. He will beam with joy as he watches his coworkers eat extremely his sweet brownies, wiggling their eyebrows in joy and telling him that he has great baking skill. If you want the baker to love you, just ask for the recipe, and write it down, then admit that you were too intimidated to try it.

The Lackey

The Lackey finds the person in his food-chain with the most power and then seeks a way to ingratiate himself to that person and to stay that way. The Lackey can be confused with the Schemer, but they are significantly different. Where the Schemer strives to make things happen while appearing to be uninvolved or neutral, the Lackey is directly involved with the boss, tirelessly and without shame. The Schemer hopes to pull strings from behind the curtain; the Lackey is running behind the boss to carry her briefcase, suggest a restaurant, buy her a birthday present, or compliment her clothes. The Schemer is horrified by the Lackey's open groveling, feeling that such things should be done quietly and tastefully. The best way to get along with the Lackey is to never get between him and the boss; allow him to grovel freely. He will not make any serious moves and does not require much of your attention.

The Secret Agent

The Secret Agent has her own agenda. She will not stay forever like a Lifer, does not curry favor like a Lackey, seems to be above the conniving of the Schemer, and could not be bothered bringing in a baked good. As for the Neurotic, the Secret Agent avoids this person at all costs, since they may accidentally attract attention to the Secret Agent with their neurotic flailing around. The Secret Agent is not difficult to get along with; just don't accidentally disrupt their plans – the rage is frightening. If you do make such a blunder, don't let it fester – have a brief conversation with the Secret Agent about the misunderstanding. The content of the conversation does not really matter – you are only showing the Secret Agent that you are harmless.

Jones put the book in his lap and looked up at Moe and Moran. "This is pretty good stuff, but I am not sure about the 'Secret Agent' as a separate type from 'the Schemer.' I know you said that the motivations are different, but I think motivations are difficult to discover. I recommend that you combine the "Secret Agent' and 'the Schemer' – of course, I am not your publisher."

Doctor Moran was quick to reassure Jones that his comments were not only welcome, but earnestly solicited and highly valued. Jones smiled, stretched his arms over his head, leaned back in his chair and said, "Well then, let's talk compensation for my services."

Moran said, "What, more ham and cheese sandwiches?" Jones said, "No, I'm still full from the alien paste you gave me earlier -- just kidding. Moran, why do you still look like a man if I know now that my assumptions were wrong? Are you going to change into a woman at any point? Are the first assumptions locked in place forever?"

Moran said, "Stop obsessing about my gender and appearance. Yes, your assumptions became 'locked-in forever' as your call it. You do not need to know what I really look like, do you? Can you not just have a conversation, read our book, and treat us like human beings? Please! Read on – MoeJoe is very proud of this chapter."

Moe said, "I would not say that I am proud of it, but it was great fun doing the research."

THREE ENVIRONMENTS

Cubicle Wastelands

Florescent lights, low walls, synthetic materials, dirty carpet, dust, mold, sneezes bouncing off the walls, 'acoustic' ceiling tile. Bonus: This environment gives you a strong sense of post-apocalyptic doom, which adds authenticity to the experience of reading those novels or watching those films. If you can sit in your desolate break area and read some of those books, the feeling will be intensified. If you can sit in your break area, read the book, drink bad coffee, and start divorce proceedings, you may just morph into a giant insect.

Walnut-Look Panels

A 'cut above' the Cubicle Wasteland, this environment sports wood-finish doors and furniture,brass-toned door handles, and better carpet. The ceiling tiles are still glued-together dust and the occasional offices are really just high-walled cubicles with doors and false ceilings, but oh the luxury! Bonus: You can pretend that your life has meaning to the corporation. Don't do this for more than five minutes a day or you could start to believe it.

Cinderblocks Covered with Carpet

This is the new style of workplace that wants to be 'cool' and iconoclastic. The idea is that a workplace should look like a "play-place" and everyone will be happy, creative, and productive. This is just a large cinderblock rectangle, subdivided into three floors and *some rooms, walls covered with wild-patterned carpet,*

and a giant Styrofoam puzzle-cube hanging from the

ceiling in the lobby. Bonus: You can dress like a teenager

and behave in juvenile ways without attracting

attention.

Jones was impressed and said, "Moe is right
to be proud of this section – I would not change a
thing, except maybe the, 'giant insect' part. It is
uncanny how well he captured the workplaces of
our time. Great job, Moe..."

Moe smiled and saluted awkwardly and
appeared uncomfortable with the compliment.
Moran nodded enthusiastically and said, "He
really does have a great talent for capturing a time
– that is why he gets away with all his rebellious
acts. The next chapter is one that we are not sure
what to do with. MoeJoe said he was being
sarcastic to allow himself some creative outlet, but I

think there are nuggets of truth in these tips – see what you think please."

MOEJOE'S TIPS FOR SUCCESS

Use email as a weapon; that is exactly what it is for

Follow your dreams, i.e., sleep at your desk

Set goals, otherwise you will not know when you have won. "Destroying all in your path" is not a reasonable goal – who will do your work for you if you destroy everyone?

Why are you working? If you don't know why you are working, stop everything until you figure it out. Even then, why are you still working?

Leverage paranoia – it is the one trait you will never regret – allow it full control.

Jones said, "I can see why you are hesitant to delete this section – it is really quite amusing.

Still, it is generally terrible advice, so I am not sure who the audience is and whether you would actually give it to someone who will need to succeed in 21st century corporate America."

Moran and Moe looked at each other conspiratorially again and then Moran nodded and sighed. Moran straightened her posture a bit and looked directly at Jones and said, "We did not intend to tell you this much so soon, but your questions are actually very apt and we have reached this point very quickly." Moran stood and paced up and down and then resumed her seat. "This is more than a book – it is a training manual." She raised one eyebrow and looked at Jones as if to gauge how impressed he was with the sharing of this secret.

Jones shrugged and said, "So? What's the big secret – it's a training manual – so what?" Jones

looked from Moran to Moe and back to Moran. "I
don't get it. You guys are going to train some
people from this time and send them back to our
time and what? See if they can make their own
corporation and be successful doing it? Why would
you want to do that?"

Moran frowned at Jones and said, "You
know, Jones, you are actually the one who should
have a clown supplemental." She tapped the badge
at her lapel in a pattern and she was suddenly no
longer a man, but an angry woman in a cotton
jumpsuit, glaring at Jones. "We are going to
infiltrate a corporation in your time, then operate
one in our own time. No, it is not easy or obvious –
it will take a great deal of work and planning. It
will be dangerous, in fact, given the violent and
reactionary world that you inhabit."

Jones said, "Well, back to reading! Please don't mind me – I will just be absorbed in this book for a few minutes, then providing you with serious and well-considered feedback." Jones made a mental note to tell Moran at some later, more opportune time, that she was very attractive, especially her eyes, but he was sure that this was not the right time. He appeared as studious as he could, given the fact that he did not make such an expression very often, and began reading, still aloud, but not smirking this time.

THE 5 TYPES OF LEADER

The 4 Star General (TFSG)

This person thinks that leading is synonymous with charging, so that's all they do – all day long. They think of a work as a hill that needs to be charged, with much loss of life (someone else's of course) and a medal for the survivors.

Jones said, "This is good, but not very helpful for the reader. You need a section called,

"How to deal with the Four-Star General" and all the other types you will discuss – otherwise, what good is it to just identify them?"

Moran seemed surprised and said, "That is actually a good point, Jones, thank you." Jones said, "Thanks, but I noticed that whenever you say anything good about me, you use the word 'actually' as if it is a big surprise."

Moran said, "Do I? Sorry about that. Anyway, the problem is that we do not really know how to deal with these types; we do not have enough experience with them. MoeJoe is comfortable identifying and classifying them, but he could not advise people on how to approach or manage them."

Jones, anxious to return to grace, said, "I can tell you for each of these, what to do to handle them – I may not have risen to CEO, but definitely know how to survive in the corporate fishbowl. For example, here is what I would say about the TFSG."

"**How to Deal with TFSGs:** Avoid the temptation to speak in short sentences with a stern expression on your face – this will only encourage the General to act more authoritarian. While the General is giving you an order, smile broadly and look vacant. The General will eventually stop and ask you what is so amusing, or, even better, will start guessing at what you find amusing. Make jokes freely, even if you are the only one who thinks it is funny. This taps into the huge well of insecurity that the General is attempting to overcome and will completely derail the power trip of giving you orders."

Jones noted with some gratification that Moe and Moran seemed impressed with his impromptu suggestions on how to deal with the general. He returned to reading.

Saint with a Hangover (SWAH)

This leader has read too many books about leadership and perhaps has attended too many business workshops and lectures. SWAH wants to be humble, open, collaborative, creative, and just plain nice to be around, but is usually grumpy and passive-aggressive.

Jones was impressed and amused by the name and said, "Saint with a hangover – very good. So you really do know your history; such a nice reference that people of our time would actually get; so colorful – the incongruity of the hangover and the saint. Here is my suggestion of, **How to Deal with SWAHs.** Take this person at their presented persona and force them to live up to it. Tell them as often as possible that you appreciate their open leadership style and that you treasure their openness to new ideas. If they become annoying by trying to give you work or judging your work, bombard them with idealistic proposals that have no chance of success. Describe your ideas with passion and excitement, then sit back and watch SWAH repeatedly crashing against the walls of corporate apathy."

Jones noticed Moe scribbling furiously on a legal pad – trying to get all these ideas down. Jones asked, "Why are you guys still using pen and paper? Don't you have all sorts of amazing brain-computer interfaces that make transcription much easier?"

Moran smiled, "Yes, we do, as a matter of fact, but MoeJoe is a re-enactment buff – he likes to practice doing things the way they were done in his period of specialization. He sometimes takes it a bit far, in my opinion, such as when he drinks bad coffee and squints at an old-time computer screen for hours, eating chocolate candies and getting a stiff neck." Moe just laughed and kept jotting on his pad. Jones continued reading.

The Angry Child (TAC)

This leader feels unsatisfied and incomplete and will not notice you until you either:

a. *Annoyingly ask for something, reminding them of all the things that they do not have,*

(Or)

b. *Annoyingly raise your head from the drudgery of your work to say that you have no more capacity for additional assignments, reminding them of the fact that you are an actual organism that has limitations, which will again remind them of all the things that they do not have.*

Jones whistled in admiration and said, "You guys have really done your homework. The workplace is littered with 'Angry Children' and most people have not noticed that they are a phenomenon of the modern workplace ... well 'modern' in our sense. This one is actually relatively easy to deal with – their 'button' is so obvious, once you know where to look."

"**How to Deal with TACs**: Ask for at least one thing that you do not want every day. This will keep TAC in a constant frenzy and keep him away from your desk. Further, when you finally do want something, offer it as an alternative, much less preferable than your original request; it is even better if you can get TAC to propose the alternative, which you will grudgingly accept. TACs love flattery and attention, but this will probably make you sick, so proceed with caution. TACs will take whatever you have that you seem to enjoy or receive praise for, which provides an infinite source of entertainment. For example, ask for the company to pay for a course in advanced statistics, which you will say is your lifelong dream. TAC will deny your request and then find justification for TAC to take the course himself – for which TAC will obviously suffer unbearable torment and regret."

Moran frowned and said, "I don't get the 'advanced statistics course' reference – I guess my knowledge of your time is not as comprehensive as you kindly suggested. I have not uncovered any statistical methods from your time that would qualify as advanced. MoeJoe, do you get it?"

Moe smiled and nodded and said, "Yes, in this period, the significance of data was calculated in ways that have long-since been discredited and abandoned. The methods were very close to 'brute-force,' alternating with assumptions bordering on mysticism. With the advent of the personal computer, this became much worse and the corporate world became inundated with meaningless and misleading measurements and conclusions. Even people who promoted themselves as experts kept forgetting the principles of the discipline, since they were arbitrary. So, the course would be torture."

Jones laughed and said, "That was harsh! I guess historians can get away with all sorts of scathing judgements – I really like that approach." He continued reading.

The Simpering Psychotic

This person is like SWAH, except they do not know all the modern management theories and trendy practices; they just noticed at an early age that they could get more out of people by being "nice." They actually detest the human race and would not care if you

were dipped in boiling oil and roasted on a spit. Yet they

smile! Oh how they smile at you! They ask you all about

your personal life in the most honeyed tones; all that you

say with a smile is worth a laugh from them! Oh you are

so witty and endearing and such a pitiful little worker-

elf skipping around doing whatever it is that you do with

your family, but could you please just skip off a cliff?

Jones was unable to contain a burst of laughter upon reading these bitter remarks, glancing at Moe who also seemed to be enjoying himself. Jones glanced at Moran, but she was not smiling, so he guessed that Moe had gotten a bit 'creative' with this one and had begun to annoy Moran with his use of 21st century vernacular. Jones said, "Okay, very well done, but this one is, as the name implies, a dangerous adversary, so my recommendations will be complicated, by necessity."

"**How to Deal with TSPs:** The TSP is a control-obsessed tyrant with a poorly-fitted mask, displaying a manic smile. TSPs have managed to deceive even themselves, which makes them especially creepy and dangerous." Jones paused and looked at Moe and Moran with his most serious face, then continued, "The TSP will always uncannily consider the audience, even eavesdroppers. Show the TSP multiple personalities of your own. In conversation, rant about restaurant service or the phone company, showing bitter sarcasm and completely disproportionate rage. Let the conversation end in that manner, glinting and jaw-clenched. In the next conversation, laugh about everything; shake your head in good-humored amazement at this carnival called, "Life." When the TSP mentions past anecdotes and the names of your family members, show complete bafflement: "Who?" "What story?"

"When did I tell you that?" The TSP will become very afraid of you and minimize contact with you, which should be exactly what you want." Moe and Moran nodded cautiously and glanced at the book again, as if to say, 'please keep reading,' so Jones read on.

The Hairy Chest (THC)

In spite of the name, this leader can be of either gender. THCs pride themselves on the fact that they never sought management, they were just damn good at what they did and promotions followed. They are loud, bullying, sometimes jolly, "Let's roll up our sleeves and get it done!" kind of people. THCs emphasize their capability and practicality because they have no ability to think strategically. They run around in a frenzy in the misguided hope that 100 tactical decisions will equal one strategic decision. Not that they know the difference between tactics and strategy, just that they have a queasy feeling that they are supposed to be less hands-on *and more managerial. Needless to say, they are the most annoying of the 5 types and you will be hard-pressed to tolerate them for more than a week.*

Jones was beginning to enjoy being treated as a subject matter expert and he began to assume a wise and world-weary expression as he tackled the next manager type. "This is a tough one – this can easily go wrong if not handled correctly."

Jones said, "Anyway, **How to Deal with THCs:** Whenever THCs assign work to you, contradict you in a meeting, or find fault with work you have submitted, push the **'Big Headache Button."** Push this button by asking, 'What is the long-term goal? What is the overall strategy that we are executing toward? What are the tactical steps in this plan and how do they lead to accomplishment of the strategy?' ...Oh the head pain! Oh the misery of having a gadfly worker such as you! Once again, your manager will become very afraid of you and minimize contact with you... which is excellent!"

Jones then said to Moe and Moran, more quietly, "This is probably a good place for a footnote, with a quote for your reader, such as, 'You must not fight too often with one enemy, or you will teach him all your art of war.' This is from Napoleon."

Moran said, "Napoleon Bonaparte also said, 'Men are more easily governed through their vices than through their virtues' ... that might be appropriate somewhere as well."

Jones raised his eyebrows and said, "Your knowledge of history is astounding – I only have to toss around a few nuggets from times of my choice to look like I know something, but you just went back 5 centuries and you were responding to something I chose to mention – I doubt that I just happened to stumble upon your specialty."

Moran smiled and said, "I never said I was a fool – that must have been something you "assumed"… not to re-open old wounds."

Jones was glad to see that Doctor Moran was beginning to smile, from the entertainment of taking a jab at him, which was well worth it, since the mood was lightening.

Jones took the opportunity to ask a few questions about the planned company. "So when you start your company in your time, will you have to interview and hire people from my time -- let's call them '21s,'- or are you going to make the whole company out of '24s'? If they are all 24s, then you will need them to spend a long time in the 21st century, before they try this in the 24th."

Moe said, "You are exactly right; we have talked for hours about this very dilemma; we thought about having a mix of 50/50 - 21s and 24s, but that would mean uprooting many 21s and bringing them here, possibly against their will. There really is no perfect answer. I have some experience with 21s now, as you know, and I feel that I can safely pass as a 21. I can also train my fellow 24s in some of the fundamental aspects of blending in, but there are many skills and even an attitude toward life that cannot be taught – it must be experienced for oneself."

Moran nodded and said, "Yes, and you are right, Jones, that outsiders, such as vendors and contractors could easily notice some difference and it could spiral into some sort of witch hunt or 'alien wars' or whatever violent spasm your time might go through. We are going to have to train our people well, both to find a job, and to keep it without attracting too much attention."

Jones said, "Right, well, I see you do have a chapter called 'Interviewing,' so I will skip over to that part and review that for you."

INTERVIEWING

The Candidate

If you have the opportunity for an interview, such as a chance for a promotion, where the hiring manager is from the 'host time,' you will need to know the following facts:

STEPHEN MCLOUGHLIN

1.   An employment interview is an advertisement. As with any advertisement, it is more than 80% visual. So dress and groom extremely well ... and smile.

2. *A consumer of an advertisement makes an initial judgement in the first 50 milliseconds, so will the interviewer.*

3. *A resume is just your ad copy – it will be scanned across the top, then a bit lower for the most recent job, then at the bottom of the last page, just as a ruse to indicate that the interviewer read the entire document.*

4. *By now, the interviewer is looking for justification for the judgement that he or she has already formed, so relax, there is nothing you can do.*

The Hiring Manager

The hiring process is just like the interview process, only you are the interviewer and so you should behave as you see above, making a snap judgement within moments of seeing the candidate and then reviewing the resume only to confirm the judgement that you have formed. There are 'best practices' and

'rules,' however, some of them legal. For the legal rules,

see our appendix, but the 'best practices' are:

1. *Make sure the interview takes at least 30*
   minutes, regardless of your decision.

2. *Take notes scrupulously; you can toss them*
   later.

3. *If you are still undecided about the candidate,*
   tell them the formal interview is over, but keep
   chatting about random things about life and you
   will see more of the true candidate.

4. *Never forget that nothing on the resume and*
   nothing that the candidate says contains any
   certainty of authenticity; it's just an
   advertisement.

Jones nodded in appreciation and said,
"This is all accurate as far as it goes, but do 24s

really know how to work? I mean, what are your actual skills? You will be competing with people who have no 'assumption filters,' no 'endless supply of energy,' and no time machines... it could be rough."

Moe started to speak and Jones said, "Oh, I know *you* do Moe, or 'Hamby,' because you do it today, but running a company that makes money and buys stuff and makes more money and has insurance and pays benefits and unemployment ... I just don't know how you are going to do it. Maybe it will be more of a hybrid of our time and yours?"

Moran and Moe exchanged another one of their loaded glances and Moran asked, with a truly charming dimpled smile, "Jones, you have been so helpful! Are you sure you don't want to take a break, have something to eat and drink, maybe walk around the facility or get some fresh air?"

Jones said, "That is an excellent idea! Afterward, you can tell me what it is that you are slowly nudging me toward and what's in it for me. Oh, and tell me your first name – I think we should be that familiar by now."

Doctor Moran said, "Wonderful, I will order whatever you want to eat and drink and we can have a meal together in the lab canteen. After that, I will take you on a little walk around the grounds. … My name is Nicola – friends call me Nicki." Jones noticed that 'Nicki' did not address the fact that he said she was manipulating him for some hidden purpose.

Moe excused himself with some comments about needing to get back to the lab. Jones started to ask if he would be missed at work back in the 'good old 21st century,' but then realized that it would sound ridiculous to people who could select any time that they wanted to visit. Doctor Moran stood up and picked-up another, larger book. Moe left and Jones stood up to follow Moran to the canteen. As they left, Jones looked back at the office and watched Moran closing the door. She caught up with him and asked, "What is it?"

Jones said, "I just would have thought that the concepts of 'office' and 'rank' would have become obsolete by now, yet you have an office and Moe works in the lab. It is still hierarchical. Moe seems to report to you and defer to your decisions – it's a bit disappointing, actually."

Moran laughed and said, "I bet! You must be feeling really discouraged right now – no progress in three centuries? That's terrible!" Moran finally stopped laughing and looked Jones in the eye as they walked down the corridor together. "We have created an environment that we felt would be comfortable for someone from your time. It is, as you say, highly structured, even bureaucratic. This is not just your assumptions at work either – we have actually created this environment to do our research and we practice behaving in a hierarchical manner. MoeJoe is not my subordinate at all. I don't normally have an office – they are completely pointless now. We just did not want you, or anyone else that we bring here, to have a nervous breakdown – we needed you operational as quickly as possible."

Jones said, "Which brings me back to the question of what you really want from me – all this preparation and attention cannot just be so I could review your book."

THE OFFER

Jones had a good meal and another tasty cup of coffee and felt revitalized. This time, he did not question the source or the 'true nature' of his food – he just enjoyed it. Doctor Moran seemed to enjoy her meal as well and chose a cup of steaming jasmine tea for her beverage. When Jones finished his meal and began to enjoy his coffee, he wanted to remove his plate. He looked around the canteen and saw a metal conveyor leading into a closed space, presumably the area for food prep and

dishwashing. Jones said, "Really? We still have to take our dishes to the conveyor in the 24th century?" Moran said, "Yes, we do, in this building; please take mine with you. Is this not a good replica of the canteens in your world? Did we miss something?" Moran held up her plate for Jones to take as he passed her. "No" Jones said, "It is a perfect replica, congratulations. What do you people do with your dishes? Are they edible, a bit sweet, and you eat them for desert? Or do they evaporate after twenty minutes of use?" Moran said, "We can talk about that later, hurry back – we have much to discuss."

The lab canteen had one wall that was mostly windows, so Jones was afforded his first look at the outdoors of the 24th century. The building seemed to be surrounded by a forest of mature hardwood trees, pines, and cedars. Jones suddenly realized that this was the 24th century and so that chances of this really being a window with trees outside and blue sky were rather slim.

Jones frowned slightly and looked around the canteen, not noticing that Doctor Moran was watching him. She said, "Don't worry Jones, it's not a projection or an assumption filter disguising a bleak post-apocalyptic landscape – it really is just a large window with trees outside. Some things could not be improved upon and have not been changed. Glass windows and trees are good examples."

Jones was skeptical. "So, Nicki, what about your beautiful smile and those soulful eyes, are those real too?" Moran smiled only slightly and said, "This is the real me, but please don't try to flirt with me, Jones. It could never work between us."

Jones smiled and said, "Don't be so formal – you can call me "Jonesy" if you want to. Anyway, why are you giving me the 'cold shoulder?' How do you presume to know that I am interested in you? Why don't we go out sometime in the evening – your world or mine – and see if anything sparks-up?"

Moran shook her head, "Think about it Jones – you don't know anything about me, or the world that you are in – you are way out of your depth here. Plus, think of your age!" Moran smiled broadly and added, "I know I like older men, but 'dead for over 300 years' is taking it a bit far, don't you think?"

Jones said, "No big deal – that just means you get to call me 'daddy' whenever you want to."

Still, Jones became silent and pensive, thinking about the, 'Dead for over 300 years' remark. He sipped his excellent coffee and looked out the window at the leaves on the trees moving gently in the breeze. Moran watched him, but said nothing.

Finally, Jones broke from his meditative state and asked, "Why is this canteen empty except for us? I still don't think any of this is real; it is actually a bit creepy. I bet I am swimming in some soupy vat with a bunch of carnivorous worms and all this is some drug-induced illusion. You and your boyfriend Moe are toying with me."

Moran said, "I don't have a romantic relationship with Moe, and I noticed that you did not find this room 'creepy' until I rejected your advances. Now we're talking about 'vats' and 'giant worms' again."

Jones said, "Priorities shuffled."

Moran said, "Shuffle them again – do you want to talk about the job offer or not?"

Jones was surprised at the sudden mention of a job offer, with no preamble. It was not how things were done in his time, but he could adapt. Jones leaned back in his chair and stretched his arms behind his head and said, "I am listening, Doctor, please proceed."

Moran thought she had never seen anyone bounce from pessimistic brooding to outrageous hubris so quickly.

Moran pointed at the cover of the book she brought from her office. Its title was, *"CANDIDATE PROFILE: Sorrento Jones,"* with the subtitle *"Still Working on the Important Part,"* then lower on the cover, *"By MoeJoe the Scandalous."* Moran turned the book toward Jones and said, "Read a bit; you may be surprised." Jones slid the book closer and said,

"'*MoeJoe the Scandalous?*' Is 'MoeJoe the clown' a new name then?" Moran said, "Oh yes, MoeJoe changes identities every few days. The, 'MoeJoe the Barbarian' period was trying for all of us."

As he perused the book, Jones was indeed surprised; Moe's profile of him was highly complementary. It seemed that Moe had been analyzing him throughout his time in the company. The gist seemed to be that Jones was an excellent candidate for the CEO job in their proposed company.

Jones was called an 'agile learner who loved to learn something new,' and 'avoids spending time in his comfort zone.' He was described as 'willing to take risks.' Jones thought about Moe's persona of Hamby and how they had often engaged in heated debate while the rest of the meeting participants looked-on in horror.

Jones looked up from his reading and Moran smiled and said, "Surprised? Moe actually thinks the world of you. All the trouble he caused you was just to prove his theories of your adaptability. By the way, he is much better person than you think – not the 'weasel' that you called him."

Jones said "I don't think I like this comment that I can accept being 'the dumbest person in the room,' as long as I am learning." Moran said, "Come on, Jones! Don't be so sensitive. Moe is only saying that you can sublimate your ego get to the best decision." Jones said, "I know, but now I am imagining him in our meetings, judging me as the dumbest person in the room, which maybe I am, but isn't 'dumb' a regressive word? Shouldn't it have been tossed-out centuries ago?"

Moe had written that Jones could collaborate with anyone and was always open to new experiences and ideas – that his perspective was that 'the best idea wins,' regardless of its author.

Jones read and laughed quietly. Moran asked him, "What's funny?" Jones said, "Moe is talking about my 'thought experiments' here – I thought he found them trivial. He would just smirk and make notes and not add anything to such gems as my, "Zombie enters the room and asks for a consultation." He writes here that I can, 'Make connections across seemingly unrelated areas,' but I seem to recall him sighing and saying, "I just don't see the relevance."

Moran said, "He was testing you! Don't you see that now?" Jones said, "You love him, don't you – you are in love with Moe." Moran looked at

Jones and wondered if he was salvageable. She decided that he was and merely gestured at the book as her response. Jones said, "I know, he's a cool guy, but don't sell yourself short – you are brilliant and gorgeous – never forget that."

Moran closed her eyes and breathed deeply. She said, "Why are you so amorous? Is that in the report too? Oh, and paranoid, and jealous. Is that in there?"

Jones smiled and looked down for a moment and then returned to reading, "Oh, nice, it says I can act, 'Decisively and intuitively,' rather than, 'Constantly postponing decisions through more analysis.' Well of course – there is a diminishing return to more information – at some point you have to do *something*. Someone once said, 'Chance favors those in motion' – maybe it was General Patton." Moran said, "James H. Austin."

Jones said, "General Patton... well ... maybe you're right."

Jones turned the book over to look at the back cover and then flipped it back over and turned to the table of contents. "Oh ... that was just the summary ... there are chapters on ... "Childhood Part One, the Early Years," "Childhood Part Two - the Rebellious Phase," and "Relationships" ... oh great ... no wonder you don't want me flirting with you. That chapter is really thin. This is getting embarrassing. Surely there are no pictures... oh wonderful ... my senior high school class picture survived me by hundreds of years. It should have been destroyed on the spot. Look at the caption! 'Jones shows an open and naïve gaze here, with that glaze of daydreaming that remained with him throughout his life.' Moe went too far with that one!"

Moran laughed, "You were cute and innocent then. Anyway, he is right – you do still have a faraway look in your eyes. Moe said at one point that you act facetious and superficial to protect the deeper side of you."

Jones said, "Or, quite possibly, I act facetious and superficial because the deeper side of me is generating all sorts of antagonistic feelings toward the world which I am manifesting in a pseudo-humorous manner to avoid full-blown confrontation."

Moran nodded, "Possibly and, in fact, the two theories are compatible."

Moran straightened her posture and moved her teacup to position the handle at exactly ninety degrees and said, "No doubt you would be content to talk about the deep look in your eyes for the rest of the day, but I am a direct person. We want you to run our test company. We are offering you the position of CEO and we are prepared to pay you a salary competitive with similar positions in your world. You have no relationship ties to your world, as discussed in that chapter, and you could adapt better to a three hundred year jump than anyone we have studied."

Jones tended to laugh loudly when surprised. "CEO? Are you crazy? I am the original insouciant worker, doing the minimum and now-and-then showing flashes of brilliance just to confuse my detractors. How could you possibly want me to run your company? Are you people not serious about this project?"

Moran was not discouraged by Jones' reaction. She shook her head and smiled, thinking that he was occasionally quite likable. "We have much more perspective on this than you do Jones.

The hierarchical style of business management that ruled in your time was destined to be completely discredited and abandoned within twenty years of what you call 'today.' The rapid development of artificial intelligence was only part of the change."

Jones said, "I guess information became available increasingly faster and in increasing volume."

Moran said, "Yes, it did, but it became increasingly more difficult to keep secure, until there was a sort of implosion in which all information became instant, but highly contaminated and therefore near-useless. The individual became ever more powerful and intermediation became unnecessary. Whole companies were run by one person with a handheld device; she never saw her workers and had no office. Sometimes even *she* did not exist, but was created by the collective, as a sort of figurehead. All these things had begun in your time, but were not noticed sufficiently. In so many companies people practiced no trade, manufactured no product, served no clientele, but were, nevertheless, paid professionals. Companies were making a profit in spite of massive staff redundancy, constant mismanagement, bitter sabotage, and low productivity. No one knew what the they were doing – everyone just changed the subject to what they knew, regardless of its applicability or utility. How long could it all last? Only leaders with your type of crazy adaptability survived."

Jones said, "'Crazy adaptability' is a bit strong – I prefer 'unorthodox' adaptability if you don't mind."

Moran looked intently at Jones. "I am serious here – are you familiar with 'Colony Collapse' in honeybee colonies? It is happening to bees in your time, so you should be." Jones said he had heard of it, but was not sure what it involved.

Moran said, "Colony collapse happens when worker bees abandon a hive. There is still food and the queen is still there with her larva, but all of the worker bees are gone. The larvae are still alive and developing and there are some nurse bees there, but no workers. The hive eventually dies without the workers."

Jones leaned back in his chair and studied Moran's face. "So are you saying that this is what's happening here – to people? You are losing your worker bees because they are traveling in time to get to have the fun of working?"

Moran frowned, "You are making light of it, as usual, I see, but yes, that is exactly what I am saying. We can model existing trends and forecast eventual colony collapse."

Jones said, "The good news is that you don't need workers because there really is not much work to do anymore, right? … Capital beat labor!"

Moran shook her head, "The problem is not that we need 'workers' exactly, but that we need people -- regular human beings. We have not discussed this much, but there are actually only about 3,000 people left in the world. I think the population of your time was 7 billion or so. Obviously depopulation was not a problem for you."

Jones grew serious for a moment. "3,000? What happened? War? Famine? Pollution?"

Moran shook her head, "No, while all of those things did become huge problems and did threaten the survival of the planet, we overcame all of them. We still had a few million people left. Now it is simply that people are abandoning our time. It is like a virus or some sort of bacterial plague. No one wants to be here anymore. We have to do something to keep them here and to keep our world alive."

Jones asked, "Why don't you just bring Attila the Hun and a few thousand of his tribe here and stick them in some nice, secluded spot and let them breed like crazy until things are nicely up to par again? Just pull some people in from another time!"

Moran smiled sadly, "I wondered how long it would take before you would become annoying again. Actually, we did talk about such measures,

only not a barbarian warlord and his followers –
more some other relatively peaceful people who
could live off the land and were known for having
large families."

Jones said, "You know, it's funny how you
tell me things in little pieces, slowly getting to the
point. I can't tell if you are being gentle with me, or
gentle with yourselves."

Jones studied Moran for a few moments
and then slapped his left palm on the table. "I get
it! You lied – you and Moe are the only two people
left in the world! You planned to repopulate the
world, but Moe is sterile, so you brought me! Nicki,
I am flattered! I would be happy to help you! We
have to plan this though – what shall we call the
first baby? 'Nick' it it's a boy and 'Sorrenta' if it's a
girl? Will they use filters, or do we want them to

grow-up old-fashioned? How many babies can you bear – can you have multiples to speed this up?"

Moran watched Jones in amazement and began laughing. "You are not really sane Jones, I want you to know that … not that it matters for our purposes, as long as you do a good job. No, we did not bring you here to breed and no, I am not interested in having your children and no, Moe and I are not the last people on Earth. We did not 'pull people in from other times' as you call it because it is a violent abuse of their rights as human beings."

Jones started to interrupt, but Moran said, "No, do not compare that to us bringing you here. We did the minimum disruption that we could do – and I think it will be to our mutual benefit."

Jones was still puzzled and said, "There is something about this plan that I still don't get … I accept your offer by the way, it should be fun –

why do you think running a successful company in your time will help you with your 'colony collapse' problem?"

Moran nodded and said, "I know, it is not an obvious remedy, but stay with me for a moment. The people who move to your time to work will be preserved. Then, once they are ready, we will bring them back here and start our company. We will turn-off the assumption filters that provide the commodity in our time and we will begin to produce it *here*. Then we will begin adding other products, gradually not producing them in your time at all, once we have enough workers to produce the items here. Since we can sometimes manipulate time, we hope to make all of this happen quite quickly."

Jones leaned back in his chair and exhaled and said, "Now I finally get it. The assumption filters are a big flop. Everyone is sick of them, but people don't know how to get by without them. The core infrastructure is ugly and would drive away the remaining people from your world if you just turned off all the filters. You are going to try to gradually return to how life was before the filters. What happened to all your smug comments about only consuming 1% of what we consume?"

Moran decided that she really did not like Jones at all, not even when he seemed humble and self-aware, as he had for a few seconds when she first offered him the job. Jones saw her serious gaze and sobered-up and said, "Sorry, don't stew about it, looking at me like you really hate me. I was just teasing you! I know your problem is serious and will require serious measures. I too want the human race to survive, even if I am not as personally committed as you are. I mean, I can go back where I came from, but I guess you wouldn't consider deserting this world and coming to mine? I will help you to blend in and find a comfortable way of life – you can even bring Moe."

Moran stopped glaring and said, "That is a kind offer, but no, I will not leave my world in this bind, and neither would Moe. Most people have grown up with the Assumption Filters and really know no other way of living. This is going to be a very difficult transition – if it succeeds at all."

Jones smirked and said, "So, we need the proletariat after all – Marx would be so proud. Okay! Sign me up! What sort of benefits do I get? Can I go on sick leave tomorrow? This time travel has left me with some sort of chill."

Moran tapped her badge and said, "I'm calling Moe – you guys have a lot of work to do." Moe came striding in a few seconds later, looking exactly like a past president of the United States from Jones' time. Moe, in his navy blue suit, white shirt, and yellow tie, crossed the room with his hand extended and a friendly smile. Jones started to stand up and caught himself just in time.

A FEW GLITCHES

Moran said, "Hello Mr. President!" and batted her eyelashes at Moe. Moe said, "Hi boss – why are you batting your eyelashes at me?" and winked at Jones. Moran said, "That's for Jones – he has an obsession that I am feeding, don't ask me why. By the way, President MoeJoe, Jones has accepted our offer; please start the cerebral restructuring procedure."

Jones said, "Wait a minute! He then realized that Moran was joking. Jones laughed and said,

"Oh, so you actually have a sense of humor buried in that spectacular mind! So glad you let it out of its cage for five seconds before slamming it back inside. Please don't kick it as you close the door – it really meant no harm." Jones turned to greet Moe and said, "Hey Pres, nice book – thank you for your kind remarks; I have a death grudge against you for that high school photo; why the subtitle about 'the important part' – what's that about?"

Moe said, "That's from you, Jones! When I first began working in your department, I asked permission to spend a few hours with each manager to learn what they did for the company and what their challenges were and so on. You told me something funny – that to be successful one needed to be smart enough to be good at it, but dumb enough to think it was important. You added that you were still working on the 'important' part. You even made a Venn diagram. I thought that was hilarious."

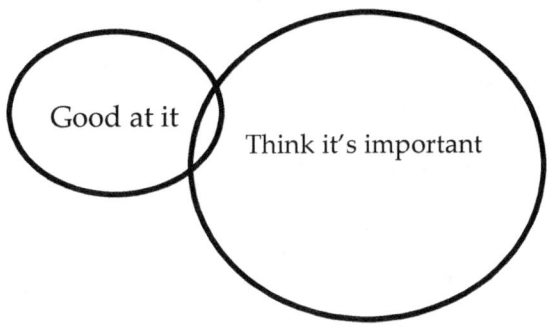

Moran said, "The first part of that quote is a paraphrase of a quote from a United States Senator." Jones said, "I think it was a comedian, but maybe you're right." Moran said, "The last part is classic Jones." Moe said, "Yes, I wrote that down, thinking, "This guy is great – I can learn from this man!"

Jones laughed, "You know, I would have expected people of this time to be arrogant little weaklings, floating around in pale halos and never saying anything sincere or direct. If you two are any indication, people are now more sincere than they were in my time… better looking, too."

Moran nodded and said, "Good observation about sincerity, Jones. In fact that is true - people express themselves more authentically than they did in your time. As I mentioned earlier, the concept of truth lost all value before the end of your century. Sincerity did not appeal to the lowest common denominator – cynicism did. When all sincerity is lost from communication, what is left? Just verbal games, bantering, memes, facetious posturing…"

Jones said, "I think you are insulting me, but don't worry about it. I need some fresh air, can we walk in that little grove of trees out there, or is it all radioactive? If I have to wear a special suit, or I will wither within seconds of stepping outside, just let me know now."

Moe stood up and said, "As the leader of the free world – I can assure you that our beautiful outdoor environment is safe." He gestured broadly toward the long window and said, "Please, follow me." Moran said, "I will be in my office. You two go and do some male bonding."

Jones followed Moe to an exit door and asked as he walked, "Did she get that cheesy 'male bonding' expression from my time, as an artefact, or do people still say it all these hundreds of years later?" Moe said, "Oh, that's more mischief from the Assumption Filter. The filters take our language and translate it to the language from the time of the listener. Doctor Moran said something vaguely analogous to 'male bonding' and the filter did the rest."

Jones said, "What would happen if you brought two people from my time who spoke two different languages, say me and a Chinese woman – which language would the filter use?"

Moe laughed, "You do ask good questions, Jones – I have always said so. The filter is more complex than it first appears. It is not just a thing stuck on the speaker and sending out one signal – it is a machine-human interface that interacts with all counterparties. You would hear your language and the Chinese speaker would hear Chinese."

They stepped outside into fresh air, a beautiful breeze, and the scent of pine and cedar trees. Moe stopped and took a deep breath. Jones stood beside him and found himself doing the same. It was such a relief to be close to nature after such a disorienting experience. Even though Moran and Moe had done a great job of replicating his world, it was not a perfect job and there were nagging differences in the periphery.

Jones took the opportunity to ask Moe a question that he had postponed, given Moran's frequent displays of annoyance with him. Jones said, "A few minutes ago, Moran said, something like, 'We can sometimes manipulate time' and that you, 'Hope to make this happen quickly. This sounded like the time travel thing is not entirely perfect. What was that about?"

Moe glanced toward the window of the cafeteria, but Moran was gone. He seemed to be missing the usual nod they exchanged that showed an agreement that something could be disclosed. Moe sighed and then said, "There are some bugs in the time travel methodology. The use of the 'Uncertainty Principle' has added more uncertainty than we hoped. Essentially, we cannot accurately and consistently predict where were we will land, neither in time nor in location. We have a team of about 200 people working full-time on the problem – it is obviously very dangerous."

Jones said, "So how do you keep coming back to my time and why are you so sure you can start and run a company in my time?"

Moe said, "Once a particular machine has been to a particular time and place, it becomes analogous to a well-worn path – it keeps going back there - whether we like it or not. Once we saw your time, we thought it would be better to go forward about five more decades, to when work was more progressive, but the die was cast. We tried a different machine and I found myself in a deep forest, in winter, with some very capable-looking warriors surrounding me. We decided that the 'well-worn path' was fine."

Jones smiled at this thought and said, "So it's no wonder Moran did not like my suggestion of pulling people here from a different time – you are not even sure what you would get."

Moe seemed surprised and said, "So she told you about the colony collapse theory. Well, it is real and it is a big worry. There is also an ethical code for the use of time travel and it is something we abide by in the strictest terms."

Jones said, "Glad to hear it. Anyway, now I understand why you cannot just go back in time to when you got into such a mess and do things slightly differently – sort of 'tune' the outcome. You are not sure you could get to the right time in the first place."

Moe simply said, "Right" and gestured at a meandering path through the trees. "Shall we stroll?"

Jones agreed and as he walked, said, "So these 'time tourists' that are bailing-out from your time and going to other places and times – they could end-up anywhere and anytime..."

Moe said, "It is a worry, certainly – we are not sure how many have survived. Still, people will not stop doing it despite the warnings. Some have found a good spot and returned to this time, then made a lot of money escorting people back to that same spot."

Jones did not see the problem. "So what if people don't listen to warnings? What warnings, anyway – that they might end up in the wrong place or time?"

Moe put his hand on a pine tree and felt the rough bark for a few moments, seemingly considering his answer and then said, "That and other things. There is another defect in our time travel that they are choosing to ignore; a particular machine has a lifespan of about twenty uses. The more one is used to travel to a particular spot, the more likely that it will eventually become completely erratic and transport someone to a time and place that is not hospitable to human life. We avoid that problem by a simple tactic that was invented by one of the more creative 'time escorts.' We take a new machine with us inside the old machine for a few trips. Just being an inactive part of that trip makes the machine more likely to return to the old spot when it is activated. Because this method is expensive, most 'time escorts' do not use it – they just keep pushing the machines past their safe lifespans."

Jones laughed and then said, "I know, it's not funny, but have you ever had some kind of smoking time machine return to this time with like arrows sticking out of it or a dinosaur inside it, munching on some dude who went to the wrong time?" Moe looked quite serious when he said, "We have now entered the realm of classified information, I am sorry to say. I cannot discuss this any further."

Jones shrugged and picked up a pinecone that had fallen near the path, nestled in pine needles. He examined it carefully, but it looked just like a pinecone from the 21st century. He looked around for a dead branch and found one of suitable size, and picked it up. Moe just watched him silently. Jones tossed the pinecone into the air and swung the branch like a baseball bat, knocking the cone well into the trees. Jones smiled and said "Yes, nice one - a double!"

Moe picked up a pinecone and held out his hand for Jones to pass him the makeshift bat. Jones did and Moe repeated Jones' baseball action, but widely missed the pinecone. It fell to the ground like a shot bird and Moe looked at Jones. "That is harder to do than it looks – I will need some practice."

Jones was horrified, "You don't have baseball anymore? Are you kidding me? Baseball? You lost baseball? Why are you people even trying to save your useless civilization?"

Moe was overwhelmed for a moment by Jones' passion. Here was a man who had shown no reaction to all sorts of bizarre differences, remained cool during Moran's scathing comments, was nonchalant about the possible end of the world, and now he was ranting about baseball? Moe sat on a weathered wooden bench near the path and Jones sat beside him.

After a few moments of silence, Jones said "Hey, a squirrel! It looks like ours! I would have thought that you guys would genetically engineer them, 'make some mistakes,' accidentally allow them to escape from the lab, and regret to tell me that they are now as big as Labrador retrievers and have teeth like saber tooth tigers."

Moe looked at Jones for a moment without speaking and then said, "Did Doctor Moran tell you what the population of the world is today?"

Jones said, "Yes, she did – I offered to help her establish a new race of world conquerors, but she declined, for some reason." Moe finally smiled again, but in a subdued manner. He said, "We have bigger problems than the demise of baseball, or how to reintroduce baseball to our time. We are in danger of having no world at all."

Jones looked at Moe, still with his presidential filter on, and wondered if Moe chose his filters with more method than madness. Jones said, "I know, I understand, you are dealing with priorities. Still, we are going to have to return to this subject after we get the world stabilized. I know you two think I am superficial and facetious, and maybe I am, but sometimes I have a deeper point. For example, I don't know what other sports and games you have lost, but there could be more to your 'colony collapse' than just people wanting to have real jobs."

Moe said, "Agreed. If we did not think well of you – you would not be here. I see that Doctor Moran is waiting for us – I think it is time to return to planning the new company."

THE STARTER TEAM

Moe, Jones, and Moran gathered in the
cafeteria. Moran seemed very energetic and did not
sit down, so Moe and Jones remained standing.
Moran beamed at them and said, "The Starter
Team is here! They are gathered in Meeting Room
E. They are really excited to meet you Jones!"

On principle, Jones distrusted most displays of enthusiasm, so he followed Moran, but lagged behind her and Moe. After a few steps, Moran looked back and smiled at Jones, "What's the problem now, looking for snake pits again?"

When they entered Meeting Room E, Jones saw only three people, a very elderly man, a girl of about 16, and a boy of about 14. That was it. That was the "Starter Team." Jones looked at Moran in amazement; then shifted his gaze to Moe. They both looked perfectly composed and happy. The Starter Team was sitting in a row on the other side of a rectangular conference table, facing the door, with copies of the 'training manual' in front of them. Moran and Moe sat in chairs on the opposite side and Moran gestured for Jones to sit in a chair beside her. Moran said, "Martha, Peter, David, this is Mr. Jones; he will be your trainer for the remainder of the project, then your manager once we implement the new company." The elderly man stood and offered his hand to Jones, who likewise stood and shook his hand. The man said, "I am David, and I look forward to your tutelage." The other two stood as well and shyly emulated David. Jones was still moving a bit slowly and looking slightly vague as he tried to process his surprise over the Starter Team. Moran said to them, "Mr. Jones has already made some great corrections and additions for our training manual and he will spend much more time with you, but we just wanted to introduce you for the time being. Please feel free to use your time as you see fit. We will begin more structure training tomorrow at 8 a.m."

Moran and Moe stood, so Jones did the same and said, "It was a pleasure to meet you." The three bowed slightly and softly said something similar and Jones left, still feeling that the situation was surreal. Moran and Moe led Jones back to Moran's supposed 'office' and sat down again. Moe picked-up his legal pad and said, "Jones, I have nothing so far about performance management. May I ask you some questions to get that chapter started?" Jones said, "Of course, fire away ... no pun intended."

Moe said, "The old concept of incentives and disincentives to motivate workers was completely discredited through research by the end of your century. I know that in your time, however, these are very important concepts in the workplace. I am having trouble thinking in these discredited and ridiculed terms. How can we do this to our own people, or even to 21s?"

Jones smiled, "I suspected as much – even in my own time. It seems to me that people are who they are and do what they are going to do, regardless of the 'carrot and stick' methods of performance management."

"Exactly so," Moe said, "Experiments clearly demonstrated that people's attention to detail, work ethic, and sense of accountability, were a product of a combination of genetics and upbringing. Performance reviews were shown to be completely superfluous at best and were even often harmful."

Jones said, "Yes, I know, I know, but your 'rock-and-roll Starter Team' will have to make it under the current system, so we have to prepare them. By the way, have you ever had a performance review at our company? You were there last March, so you should have gotten one then."

Moe grinned, "No, I dodged it. It seems that I had not been with the company long enough."

Jones said, "Lucky you. It's so weird. We all know whether or not we are doing well and we all know that people don't change, regardless of threats and promises – so the thing is an awkward charade. I do good job not because I am afraid or because I want a raise – I do a good job because of my own motivations. I would guess everyone else is the same. So what do you do in your time? Well, scratch that – you don't have work anymore. What did performance management evolve to before work stopped altogether?"

Moran said, "What replaced performance management was better selection, followed by empowerment and very loose management. All ratings and 'mutual goal-setting' stopped. What could be objectively measured was rewarded – everything else was abandoned. Still, we will need to teach 24s how to navigate such things in the 21st

century, so we will need some ideas from you on successfully navigating performance reviews."

Jones felt that this was an opportune time to ask his questions about the 'Starter Team.' He said, "A question for you both: This fine group of people that you have assembled to start our company with – are you not concerned that one is well-past retirement age and the other two are not of legal age to work in a corporation?"

Moe and Moran frowned and looked at each other as if the question was bizarre and they were not sure how to handle it. Moran finally made an attempt. "They will be using assumption filters, which you can help tune, so they will not have any problem being eligible to work. As far as ability, there is no doubt that they can do any job you devise for them, but you can evaluate them during training and let us know of any concerns."

Jones felt that he was going to lose the friendly feelings that had been building, but he pressed the question. "They were the only people you could get, weren't they?"

Moran sighed, "Yes, they were the only ones not planning to leave the planet. They are a grandfather and his two grandchildren. They have very nobly signed-up for our desperate attempt to save the World. Still they are very talented, energetic, intelligent people and fit for any duties you may have for them" Moran paused and swallowed and took a deep breath. "Give them a chance."

Jones said, "They are related to you, aren't they?" Moran sighed and said, "Yes, very astute of you Jones – the older man is our grandfather. The young people are our niece, and nephew. Their mother is, or was, our sister. She and her husband, the father of those children, time-traveled to what they thought was a better time and place. The idea was that they would establish a home and then bring the kids. We never heard from them again and they kept their destination a secret, thinking that I would interfere with them."

Jones said, "You say, "our grandfather" – Moe is your brother? This whole thing is just one family? The future of the planet depends on one family?"

Moran said, "Well, not entirely; there are other people here, they just need to see this starting to work and then they will join us, I hope."

Jones said, "Oh yes, the rest of the 3,000. It's a shame; they have no idea what they're missing. Anyway, the secret to a managing performance reviews, from the employee perspective, is all at the beginning. There is no point in trying to manage such things at the end, or even in the middle. If you have allowed yourself to be saddled with unrealistic goals or impossible to measure, subjective silliness, then you will get what you deserve at the end. There is no worse trap for the worker than to agree to a subjective measurement of one's performance. This puts all the power in the hand of the manager, which corrupts even a good manager. You have handed them a loaded gun and asked them not to wave it in your face. Good luck."

Moe said, "Yes, you have made that point, but how exactly does the employee manage the performance measures from the beginning? What if the manager has already decided what those are going to be?

Jones shook his head, "No, no, do not be fooled – the manager needs your acceptance of the measures in order to beat you with them later.

Especially if the manager is going to discipline you in any way, or if it will affect your pay, the manager needs the credibility of having your acceptance of the measure."

Moe scribbled rapidly on his pad and Moran looked at Jones and said, "Easy enough to say, but why would an employee agree to any but the easiest measures?"

Jones said, "Yes! Now you are on the right track. Of course the employee has to keep some credibility. It would be ridiculous to propose a goal like, 'Be at work as much as possible, unless I have better things to do that day.' No, the worker must look for that balance of credibility with feasibility. Insisting on an objective, clearly stated, measureable goal is already half the battle. After that, just make sure it's something you can accomplish without too much effort. It is wise to leave some work quietly on the cusp of completion, then set it as a goal, then finish it up."

Moe said, "What about from the management perspective though – our team may become managers at some point. Should they try to stop some of this manipulative behavior?"

Jones said, "Take it easy. 'Manipulative' is a strong word there, Moe – let's stay away from it. These are not manipulations – these are 'techniques for maintaining agency.' As for the manager, the rules are almost the same; setting goals that are specific and measurable is good for managers as well. Performance measurement is not the tool for getting rid of an undesirable employee in any case, so keeping things subjective is corrosive. The only difference for the manager is that he or she should be vigilant to keep the goals from being too easy. There are two reasons for this: One is that higher levels of management will review these goals and silly ones will damage the credibility of the manager. The second reason is that the worker will be demoralized if a manager is too simple-minded or gullible. The worker will feel that nothing that he does matters – that there is no need to apply himself, and will begin to disengage from the job. This is bad for both sides."

Moran smirked and said, "Is that what happened to you, Jones?" Jones said, "What do you mean, "happened" to me? Don't forget that you guys picked me - in fact, dragged me here without my consent – so now you want to 'throw this fish back in the lake'? Please do so - it won't bother me a bit." Moe looked at Moran in alarm and Moran shook her head and sighed deeply and said, "No, we don't want to 'throw you back' as you put it, don't be so sensitive. I was just teasing you."

Jones laughed, "Really? I'm flattered! I did not know you wanted to tease me. Oh, Nicki! Please keep it up a bit longer." Moran rolled her eyes and looked at her notebook and said, "So what will be the first product that your company produces for us?"

Book 1: Entering the Corporate World   160

THE FIRST PRODUCT

Moe and Moran watched Jones intently, their eyes twinkling with anticipation. This was obviously something they had waited for and talked about for a long time. Jones said, "Well, you have not given me much time to think about this … hmmm … maybe bombs? Tanks? Gas masks? I don't know …" He started laughing at the horrified faces of his hosts … "Ok, I'm joking; what did you have in mind? You obviously have some preferences. " Moran looked at Moe somewhat shyly and then back to Jones and said, "We miss the texture and taste of real bread – what do you think about making French baguettes?" Jones was amused by the smiles and sparkle from Moe and Moran, but was surprised. "How can you not have bread here? I had a sandwich! You could slap an assumption filter on any old thing and get bread. I admit it tasted a bit stale, but it was not bad." Moran shook her head, "No, we have never been able to get bread right, I don't know why. One day, Moe brought me a hot French baguette with butter. I was never the same. Oh, Jones, can you please make that bread for us?"

Jones was amazed at Moran's intensity on this subject, but he liked it. "Well, I suppose we could try a bakery – it's not really my field of expertise… but since it means so much to you both …" Moe jumped up and started pacing the office and said, "We have been growing wheat from some seeds that I got from your time. It seems to be doing well. The ovens are easy for us…" Jones stopped him in mid-sentence, "Hold on Moe, I have to run this company my way – I will decide if your ovens are fine or not. For all I know, you think they are fine, but actually you guys have been trying to bake bread with laser beams. Let's be careful about assumptions." Moe nodded quickly and said, "Of course, you are exactly right!" Jones smiled at his enthusiasm and looked at Moran, who was watching him with great interest. "Look at Mr. Jones! He is already beginning to be the boss." Jones said, "Hey, if I am the leader, then I better lead, right? Oh, and please call me 'Sorrento,' it sounds so nice, coming from you."

THE END

BOOK2: BECOMING HIGH POTENTIAL

HOW TO SUCCEED THROUGH PARANOIA, PESSIMISM, AND MANIPULATION

By Stephen McLoughlin

Book 2: Becoming High Potential   i

ACKNOWLEDGMENTS

Thank you Essie, Billy Nigel, Teya, and Ella

Contents

Your Paranoia is Justified

Some days, you feel as if the people who have control over your career are plotting against you, scheming to thwart your advancement, maligning your reputation, and sabotaging your efforts. You imagine them sitting in a cozy office, relaxed, their feet up, shaking their heads and laughing at your pathetic attempts to advance. They see you as one would see a mouse trying to climb out of an oily, stainless steel barrel. Firing you to put you out of your misery would be like kicking over the barrel

and crushing you. Should they do it? Not sure,
maybe …

You hear laughter from the office and when
they finally issue forth, they are still laughing and
asking each other where they should go to lunch
together. They troop out of the building with all the
energy and enthusiasm that morbid co-conspirators
always have.

I would like to tell you that you are wrong,
that there is no evidence of such sinister activity,
and that you will accomplish much more if you
look at life with a positive attitude. Sadly, this
would not be true – you are exactly right when you
fear the worst!

Add to these sad facts of life another
component: Even when you are truly just being
paranoid, based on past disappointments and
traumas, you are attracting more of the same! It
hardly seems fair! Do you know the concept that

"thoughts are things" and that you make something real by believing it? It sounds ridiculous, but it is true! Imagine that your boss is leaving for the day and, as she passes your empty chair, she looks at her watch with a frown on her face. You see this because you are returning to your desk after a quick trip to get a drink of water. You think, "Aha, my boss thinks I left early, but I am still here; she is judging me unfairly. She thinks I am unworthy of my pay." Your boss was actually thinking, "That chair is empty; I hope I am not working too late and getting caught in rush-hour traffic." Your boss sees you returning to your chair and you make eye contact. Your fear and self-loathing is communicated to her and now she DOES think that you are unworthy of your pay. If you had thought, "My boss is looking at my empty chair and thinking I am a priceless asset to the company and that had really been your conviction when you made eye contact, it would have become reality. Am I really saying that most of the time your paranoia will be true and the rest of the time your negative thoughts will make it true? Yes, sorry.

Those suddenly-lowered voices as you pass ... that smirk that you catch when you turn your head quickly to look behind you in the breakroom, that conversation that seems to suddenly stop and then change to sports or weather as you arrive ... they are like vampires passing a mirror and casting no reflection...

When you see your manager and your manager's boss sneak into an office and shut the door, casting one Mafioso glance at you as the door closes, you probably fight the impulse to fear the worst. You tell yourself that they could be discussing anything at all! They only want privacy for a chat! It could be about one of them having surgery to remove an unsightly growth in an unmentionable location!

No, sorry – it is about you and how difficult or easy it would be to remove you from the organization. It is not their fault; they are basically the T-cells of the organism in which you reside. As such, they cruise around all day, looking for cells that do not really belong in the organism and are therefore a threat to homeostasis. They then "execute" you and continue cruising around. So they make a few jokes while they are doing it, just to break the monotony or relieve the stress of an action – does that make them evil? Of course not!

You may be asking yourself how I could possibly know this to be true. After all, I do not know you or your workplace, so how could I know that your sense of foreboding and doom is justified? I can infer it from observable phenomena, just like dark material in space. Nearly all our Universe is comprised of dark material; some is dark matter, but much more is dark energy. People call it "dark" because it is not directly observable; it can only be perceived by inferring its existence through indirect methods. Scientists have to take what matter they can see and then watch it to study the effects on it from dark material and thereby know something about the properties of the dark material.

So when I see people getting browbeaten, demoralized, and thwarted at every turn by their management, I know something about that management's not-observable characteristics. The managers/T-cells are producing easily-observed effects, no matter how they may smile and wave from their doorways.

So how did you trigger these T-cells? How did you become recognized as an invasive or otherwise harmful cell? Everyone in your corporation is already either on top, high potential, or marked for eradication. If you were on top, you would not have time to read this book.

If you are getting eradicated even as you read this book, do not cry during the termination session! There will be other jobs; crack a joke; at least you are alive and free; next time you will be ready, because you will have read this book. So how do you become the high potential employee? Read on my friend; it is possible after all.

Is it possible that you could be successful without this book? No, you will only suffer more, due to the illusory hope that you will wallow in for a few days. It will be like you escaped from jail, leaving your cage and rushing out the door into the street, running down the cobblestones, glancing back over your shoulder, feeling some hope that you might escape. Your hopes sink when you notice that your pursuers are smiling and following you at a distance, not in any hurry. The "street" is actually a movie set, enclosed in a larger jail. You sink to the ground, sobbing and shaking your head, "No, no, please no…" So don't try it.

The High Potential Employee

In "The Master Manager," we showed you how to move from an ordinary manager into a top executive. Many readers became executives in a very short time; some became CEOs within a matter of weeks.

But you are not a manager, or not one with any power or future and the T-cells are eyeing you. You must quickly separate yourself from the pack; by becoming the emerging leader, the identified talent, the **High Potential Employee, or HPE**.

I know - 'high potential' should be something that you *are*, not something that you become. Otherwise, we all have the potential to become high potential, which means everyone is high potential, which renders the term meaningless, which it is. Nevertheless, the high potential employee, the emerging leader; those members of the big talent pool ... those people are not born; they are made.

You want to be one of those people, right? This guide will take you directly there – you actually run the risk of whiplash from the speed of the trip, *so please fasten your restraint device.* How can I be so confident? The earth is spinning at about 1,000 miles per hour and you are riding on it, so <u>you are already hurtling through space</u> – just start using that velocity to your advantage! Empty promises? Sure, but emptiness is form and form is emptiness.

First, STOP WORKING! In physics, the **Uncertainty Principle** posits that the more precisely the *position* of some particle is determined, the less precisely its *momentum* can be known, and vice versa. If your management focuses on what you are doing, then how fast you are getting there is unknowable.

Conversely, if they focus on how fast you are getting there, they cannot properly measure what you are doing! This is how the HPE can get away with doing nothing – everyone is focused on your momentum and cannot measure what you are actually doing. **The moment that what you are doing becomes obvious and measurable is the moment that your momentum no longer matters.** Read that sentence again. See? You work harder and harder and try to show all the ways that you are adding value and then you wonder why you are not recognized as high potential. You are doing it to yourself! Oh the bitterness! It's okay, stop gnashing your teeth – there is still time to rectify your **colossal** blunder.

You may say that every emerging-leader-type that you meet is a hypocritical, mealy-mouthed, sycophant who, early in life, learned that catering to the whims of those in power provided the most benefit. This type learns the company hymn and sings along at the top of their lungs, a little off-key to make sure the CEO notices. They have their own version of self-respect; it's nuanced and may be difficult to see at first glance, but it's there. [One sure sign of this type is that they answer, "I am well" when you ask them how they're doing. Who cares about grammar in such a case? Other signs are exaggerated participation in fund drives and the constant use of breath mints.]

So do you want to be one or not? If not, put this book down and make your hasty exit, we do not have time for you. Go save the world.

Are you still with us? Good, we prefer you to that sincere (remember, sincerity is a sign of pending lunacy) and awkward character, who smirked at the previous paragraph, shrugged his overly-large shoulders, shook his head slightly, and put this book down. He is destined to fail in <u>all</u> <u>endeavors</u>. In fact, we predict that within five years this young man will be abandoned by his wife, demoted twice, lose his savings on a bad investment, and get arrested in a case of mistaken identity. When he is finally exonerated and released, some nasty coworker will post his mugshot on the cafeteria wall, with the caption, *"If you see this fugitive, please alert security immediately."* Still feel so superior? We didn't think so. Oh, he left one paragraph ago.

You see, the corporate world is like a black hole in astrophysics. Note that I did not say that *all* companies are black holes – no, there is something like a, "Chandrasekhar Limit" that cannot be passed without triggering an explosion or the formation of a neutron star or black hole. Below that limit in mass, companies can be okay.

Success in the corporate world is like a 'singularity' – a point in a black hole where gravity is so intense that space, time, and so on do not work anymore - the laws of physics no longer matter. Similarly, the corporate world makes sense from the bottom, even from the middle, but as you get close to the top, none of this applies anymore.

For example, hard work matters at the bottom, output and productivity matter, even *quality* matters. In the middle, work matters less, but productivity and quality can still bite you if you do not respect those pesky requirements. At the top, however, those things do not work – in fact, they do not EXIST. Contemplate that for a moment; I did not just say that they are not *important*, or they are *in short supply* – I said that those concepts *do not exist* – they have no place in that universe.

Returning to astrophysics, singularities exist at the center of black holes, but they are protected by an "event horizon," meaning that, if you try to measure them, you cross this line (the event horizon) and get sucked-into the black hole, never to be heard from again. If you snake a trembling arm out toward the singularity with a measuring device at the end of it, the device will be measuring nothing and you will keep edging it closer and then … zip! … It is gone, and maybe your arm with it, we're not sure… probably though. All that to say that you are either in the corporate inside track or you are not, there is no way to edge up to it. You have to cross the "event horizon" and let yourself be completely absorbed by the singularity and then pop out of the other side. Like an event horizon in astrophysics, there is nothing to outwardly indicate the corporate event horizon. One moment you are on this side, next moment you are on the other side. What you will find in there is not utter darkness, though it is not exactly 'sweetness and light' either. You will find that it is missing those elements that I mentioned, such as hard work, integrity, and quality, but you will not miss them, because who really wants to work anyway?

I do not make this analogy lightly – it has the power to explain many things that have baffled workers for 'lo these many centuries.' For example, you say, "This woman came to the company straight from college only 10 months ago and she is already my boss – how did this happen? I have been here for 10 years and I have a graduate degree. How did this happen so fast?" Simple: Time, gravity, and space do not apply to the universe in which she operates. She did not get here only 10 months ago, she did not get here 10,000 years ago – there is no time at all.

You ask, "what about me? Am I not progressing?" If you are not in the HPE universe, not, you are not. Do you know those "progress bars" that appear when you are uploading a file or installing software? Did you ever notice that they are not really a reflection of the percentage of task completed, but more of a thing for you to stare at and feel better about the waste of time? They will stick near the end of the progress bar, and then suddenly finish and close. That is because they are not a meter at all; they are just filling-up and closing when the task is done – what good is that? You already know it is done – this is just a 'doggie snack' for you to toy with instead of ranting to customer service. In the same way, companies give you a sense of progress and upward mobility when you are actually going nowhere.

You say, "My coworker adds absolutely no value and yet they gave him a huge office with a window when the rest of us are crowded together in cubicles! How did this happen?" Your mistake is that you are speaking of the HPE universe as if it contains space, but it does not.

This is how the multiverse is; we cannot change it, so spare me your *weltschmerz!* Adapt and triumph.

So how do we use this knowledge to get some success? You are standing in the cafeteria line of success, clutching your dark brown plastic tray, cutlery neatly lined-up, napkin squared, alternately looking at the back of the person in front of you and then your tray, shuffling forward slowly, waiting with a vacuous little smile on your face, hoping for a big glop of corporate esteem to be ladled onto a plate and handed to you. I know that you want me to tell you how to step out of that line and walk confidently up to the front, nodding and smiling at the lucky few that you deem worth recognizing, plunging your hand in the vat of goop and rubbing it all over your face ... okay, maybe not... but read on, my friend.

When corporate executive management are beginning to notice you and to consider you for crossing the "event horizon" into their black hole of a universe, they will add you to ad hoc projects, special committees, and 'working groups' ... notice the subliminal messages, by the way – "working" group, in case you thought we were just bloviating. As the Gatekeepers begin probing you, they are secretly watching you extremely closely, out of the corners of their eyes, as it were. If you forget about "the singularity" and begin to value productivity and quality, you are sunk! That is exactly who they are screening out!

Gatekeepers are planning both to crush you and to promote you, in two equally likely and feasible plans that live in perfect balance until the Gatekeeper makes a last-millisecond decision, dictated by random and arbitrary criteria, therefore impossible to predict.

This is further complicated by "Gatekeeper Entanglement.' Gatekeepers have a sort of 'quantum entanglement' that allows them to move in perfect unison with all other Gatekeepers without seeming to communicate at all. They are really more a "Gatekeeper System" than just a Gatekeeper. Just as two entangled photons cannot be described or measured fully unless considered together, Gatekeepers are not stand-alone entities. Any measurement of a property of one of the Gatekeepers will act on that entity in some way, by collapsing a number of superposed states and will change the Gatekeeper's property by some unknown amount; which then causes the other one to change. So stop staring at them!

These Gatekeepers will have small harmless smiles and stare into space, doodle, and clear their throats randomly, but do not be fooled! They are probing you like alien doctors with stainless steel instruments. Commit the above-mentioned errors of valuing productivity and quality and you will find yourself back on the loser side of the event horizon, without ceremony and without a second chance.

Who can blame them? If you start raving about unicorns and fairies, wouldn't they consider you "low potential?" Now imagine that you mentioned these mythical creatures in every meeting... that is how you sound when you pontificate about, "Doing things right and doing the right things" or "More quality in the design stage means less quality control in production." On your old, bad side of the singularity, that was perfectly fine, and one in 654 mentions of those concepts was actually understood by someone... but not here.

The good side of the singularity has something like a home for the criminally insane, where they will send you if you keep spouting-off about quality. This quaint little asylum is where people speak in low, gentle voices and do their best to let you keep thinking you are still on the fast track. If you find yourself there, just play along and stay out of trouble – the banana pudding is actually very good – they even stick vanilla cookies in it for a special treat.

Notice that I have not said much about integrity. That is because that particular concept is even more complex and dangerous. Done badly, it does not require repeated infractions – it is a capital crime the first time it is committed. Done well, it can increase your upward speed exponentially. I should not even tell you how to do this well, because you might be tempted to try it before you are ready – if you ever are.

The trick - and I think one probably has to be *born* knowing how to do this – is to talk about doing the right thing, with an absolutely straight

face, while subliminally indicating to the
Gatekeepers that you will do everything in your
power to make sure that this "doing right" never
occurs.

No, you cannot wink, or smirk, or make a
secret sign with your hand. You cannot chuckle
when you say "right," or roll your eyes, or elbow
your neighbor. There should actually be a slight
frown on your face, as if to say, "This is serious
business and I will brook no contradiction." Yet
there must be complete confidence that you have
no moral fiber whatsoever. See? I told you this one
was tricky – better leave it for now.

If you are beginning to despair of ever
succeeding on the good side, do not be daunted!
Follow this guide and you can safely become that
emerging leader. Remember this: the black hole
naturally seeks to grow and can only grow by
absorbing more mass. You are one of those objects
of mass that the black hole wants to absorb. Black

holes in space are not just some basketball-sized aperture hanging in the darkness – there is one in the Milky Way galaxy that has the mass of 4.3 million of our own sun. It did not make it to that size by being picky about what it absorbed – so too, the corporate black hole needs you in order to grow. (Of course, the corporation will be just fine, even if you end up in the asylum, scooting down the white hallways on your bottom, wearing a paper crown and waving at the friendly keepers.)

So we have mostly talked about what does not exist and therefore what *not to do*, but what about the obverse – what should you actually do? Is it enough to simply copy the jargon, capitulate in every moral question, flatter, bribe, beg, cajole, and threaten? Certainly not, but it is a great start!

The next chapter, "Crushing the Incongruity" will give you more of what you need, but first, a note for would-be Gatekeepers.

NOTE FOR GATEKEEPER CANDIDATES

If you want to be a Gatekeeper, this book is really not for you, as clearly stated in the introduction, but I have a note for you anyway. Have you always wanted to be a Gatekeeper, spotting and developing the HPE? Do you find that being the absolute master of someone's future is a thrilling prospect? Do young people look at you with a mixture of curiosity, admiration, and disgust? You might be a natural Gatekeeper!

Is it somehow beyond your grasp though? Do you humbly try to mentor young people, only to find that a true Gatekeeper snatches them out of your hand at the crucial moment? Of course that is what happens! The path to becoming a Gatekeeper is even more complicated than the path to becoming an HPE, and that is, according to this book, a metaphysical marvel all of its own.

So how do you become a Gatekeeper? The path is not through mentorship, so stop it. Gatekeepers are not mentors; they are ruthless destroyers and creators of lives. They recognize each other instantly, as if by some third eye that only they can use and only they can see in others. The best route to becoming a Gatekeeper is to first become an HPE, then, when you have passed the gates yourself, and are ushered into the inner sanctum of power, waste no time in mentioning an HPE that you "have your eye on."

The other Gatekeepers will know that this is your candidacy to become a Gatekeeper. They will smirk at your arrogance – you only just passed the HPE test! Yet, they will respect your audacity and begin to evaluate whether they should allow you to designate an HPE of your own. This is mystical, I am sorry, but it must be so. There is no guarantee of success. Even if they allow you to designate an HPE, they will be watching for how you handle this power. Do you have just the right balance of exploitation and assistance? Can you look like a kindly grandmother when you are near your HPE, yet ruthlessly crush all independent spirit and moral compunction from them? Can you be both mother and father to them for years and then look at them as a complete stranger when the time comes to cut all ties? These and other aspects of your behavior will be scrutinized. Have courage and do your best! Bonus tip: Business Travel is very powerful. Travel legitimizes everything; that is why so many business people mindlessly travel back-and-forth across the world when they could accomplish their pretext of a reason without leaving their chair. Find an excuse to travel with the HPE even before you have been accepted as a Gatekeeper – this will help to secure your Gatekeeper status and will begin the process of destroying all annoying independent thought emanating from the HPE.

Finally, control yourself! This is not a buffet line! Stop overloading your tray and putting candy sprinkles on everything on your plate! Do not make a scene as you run from one HPE to the other; just pick one and stay calm.

Crushing the Incongruity

So here you are, on the good side of the singularity, well-versed in what *not* to do, wondering what to do so you can stay out of the asylum and pass the filters. First, let's clear the decks – casting all moral compunctions aside, so that we may focus fully on the task at hand.

You will be required to form and destroy alliances at breakneck speed, be dishonest in almost all communication (more on the exception later), and destroy careers without a moment of reflection. How is this justifiable? You ask why a book that is supposed to help you actually appears to be perfectly designed to destroy your life. Is there not a certain incongruity there? I am about to drive a bulldozer right through that wall of incongruity. Together, we are going to CRUSH THE INCONGRUITY.

So, what about karma? Can someone really act pathologically selfish and not suffer consequences from some 'universal law' or 'law of nature?' First, let me take issue with the word "pathological" – that is a loaded term – let's strike it. So, yes, you are right, karma is going to smash you later on, and there is a chance that you are going to be reincarnated as a garden slug, but let's take a calm look at that, shall we? Will you know it? Of course you will not. How do I know? Because I conducted a Thought Experiment and it told me everything I needed to know. Do not laugh at this last statement; entire philosophies have been built on the concept of thought experiments. Where would we be without the philosophical zombie, always willing to be used for one more humiliating

thought experiment?

Thought Experiment – I was a Man

When you are reincarnated as a garden slug, will you feel badly about the fact that you used to be a man, but are now just a slimy glob, oozing over a plate of dog food that was left out overnight? No way! What do you remember about your previous incarnation, right now? Were you a goat? Were you a human, but a lesser one? Were you a king, but now you are already in reincarnation decline because you were sometimes a bad king, so you were reborn as you are now, a business cipher in the 21st century? You do not know – there is a curtain between your past life and this one. So too there will be a curtain between this one and the next one, so you cannot experience any regret or existential angst about being a garden slug. See? No worries.

By the way, slugs are not so bad; they have two pairs of retractable tentacles, one for seeing and one for smelling. Gastropods in general are sexy in their own way. Also, there are parasites that live off slugs – so things could be worse.

So why do people even care? Who knows? There is also the concept of, "What goes around comes around," loosely translated to mean that your actions in this life will have consequences in *this* life. Is that true? No. All the bad things that you can think of have also happened to perfectly good people.

What about just looking in the mirror and feeling like a miserable human being and being unable to sleep at night because you are haunted by the memories of all your misdeeds and by the people you have harmed? Yes, well, there might be some of that, but 'Thought Experiment 2' will show you why none of this is really your fault – it is structural!

If you still have a hang-up about this, all you have to do is to flip a coin, deciding in advance that "heads" means you will live a moral life and "tails" means that you will be a selfish weasel. You have to be truly willing to live by the outcome. The universe will split at the moment the coin lands and in one, you will be righteous and in the other you will be a weasel. Now you can rest easy, knowing that these two balance each other.

Thought Experiment – the Life Raft

You are a passenger on a luxury yacht that begins to sink and you are directed into a life raft with the other passengers. Large letters painted on the side of the life raft state that the maximum capacity is 6, but you are ten people. As the two surviving crewmembers row away from the sinking yacht, you look out on the choppy Atlantic ocean and note that: There is no land in sight, a storm is approaching, the life raft is riding low and very close to taking on water, and there is a box of food that looks like it will last this group about 12 hours. Shark fins cut the water as they circle your boat, seagulls peck at you and beat about your

head with their wings, red ants that live in the raft crawl up your wet pants legs and bite you.

You scan all this and then find the first mate watching you as he rows. You can tell that he understands the nature of the situation and that he knows that you know. You look sidelong at the elderly passenger coughing to your right; then back to the first mate, who follows your glance.

You call out, "How far do you think we are from the nearest land?" First mate says, "Oh, about five days of rowing, if we take turns and row non-stop, day and night, and don't sink. We will certainly run out of food and fresh water before we get anywhere near land." The first mate is constantly clenching his jaw and his beady eyes seem to glow with hatred. The other crew member is the skipper; she also casts meaningful glances at the both of you and scowls at the passengers …

You did not want the yacht to sink and you did not cause it to sink; you did not choose this silly little life raft as the only rescue craft on the yacht; you did not book more passengers on the yacht than the capacity of the life raft. You did not make the thunderstorm that is approaching … none of this is your fault – it is the structure in which you find yourself.

What happens next will be partially under your control, even though nothing else has been thus far. You could dive off the boat and drown to make room for the remainder. You could volunteer to be killed and eaten in a sort of pre-emptive sacrifice. You could sidle-up to the first mate and whisper that you need to throw a few people overboard now, to save the remaining lives… there are many things you could do, or attempt to do, but none of those things is good and happy. Is it your fault that the choices are all bad? Of course not, but whether you survive is up to you. That's how the corporate world is – you did not make it, but you are in it and you do not intend to be cast to the sharks or devoured by your shipmates.

Alternatively, if you not mind being food for sharks or shipmates, you have mistakenly held this book for too long. A suggestion for you: use this book to beat yourself in the face and head, then tie it to your neck and wear it to your job like an albatross for a few months. Every time anyone asks you why you are wearing a book tied to your neck, tell them that you are an imbecile and that this book told you to do this to yourself.

Anyway, this is life in the corporate world. Your peers and everyone below you are in your life raft. The usual tactics to trim the numbers should work fine: Condemn with faint praise; appear to be at work all hours of the day and night; offer to help your coworker, and then steal all the credit and kindly report that the colleague "struggled" with the task; stamp your name on everything valuable; eradicate all trace of your presence from failures; repeat any damaging personal stories about colleagues, etcetera ... surely you must know the basics by now. This is basic blocking and tackling! By the way, that last phrase is very useful to shout angrily whenever you think you can get away with it. Use it on a subordinate who seems to be wandering toward independent thinking. They will begin to doubt whether they know anything at all without your guiding intelligence. Another good one is, "What do you think your job is, exactly?" There is no good answer to that question. Ask it of yourself, just for fun... feel that?

Thought Experiment - the Island

So I guess some people fell overboard and you somehow made it to an uncharted and uninhabited island and now there are six of you and, with no hope of rescue, it is time to make shelter, find food and water, and prepare to spend your first night on the island.

All six of you decide to stay together while you explore the island and look for fresh water, food etcetera. The island is small and it takes no time to realize that there is only a trickle of fresh water, no fruit trees, no helpless innocent mammals (except you people), and, in short, that survival will be very difficult.

You wake in the middle of the night to the murmur of voices, barely discernible over the chirping of crickets and the calling of tree frogs (hey, there are some food sources! Still, tree frogs are so cute with those little plunger feet, it will be hard to eat them).

You creep from your bed of leaves and branches and find that the first mate and the skipper are whispering together by the fire. You sneak silently closer and hide behind a tree to listen to them. To your horror, they are plotting to kill the rest of you in your beds tonight! Why? The first mate re-states his case to the skipper, but it seems more to convince himself, "We don't intend to die like the rest of them. We can't all survive – some of us have to die so some of us can live." The first mate is waving a knife around as he speaks and the skipper is nodding grimly, looking over her shoulder at the sleeping innocents. You are horrified – you thought you were the most dangerous and ruthless member of the castaways, but now you realize that you are an angel compared to these desperadoes.

You run into the dark forest, bumping into trees and tripping over roots. You hear yourself gasping for air and making little grunting and whining noises as you fall and stagger through the woods, expecting to be seized and stabbed at any moment.

Somehow, you have survived. Days have passed. You have found shelter in a cave and find it to be easily defended, as it is high in a mountain and difficult to approach undetected. You have an excellent view of the lowlands and have often seen the two crewmembers moving out below, with homemade spears, apparently hunting something or someone…

One day, while you are busy gathering firewood, they are able to catch you unaware and they yell their war-cries and fling their spears at you with deadly force. As you turn in fright, you slip and fall headlong down a slope, bouncing off rocks and finally landing far below, not sure if you are badly injured. Your attackers are visible, far above, looking for a path down, and unable to find one. The first mate sees you and meets your gaze before hurling a huge rock at you. You roll to one side and barely avoid being crushed and you watch them looking around frantically for more boulders. Struggling to your feet, you find that your bones are not broken and you stagger into the jungle, finally making your way back to your safe little cave by nightfall. You forgo a fire, since you feel that you are being stalked. You pass a cold, weary, night, remembering when your mother used kiss you goodnight and make sure you had a cozy blanket. No blanket now, my friend; try not to embarrass us with your loud sobbing.

The next day, you are very sore and stiff, but you decide to look around from the safety of your cliffs. You now know that your enemies will always be a threat to your life. Waving a white flag and seeking to make a peace treaty would be suicide - these are not the type of people who would honor a flag of truce. You go exploring again; there must be a way to catch them unaware!

You spot them, moving about far below in a garden – yes a garden! It turns out that they had seeds and a desalination kit and are growing carrots and cabbages. You, on the other hand, are malnourished and desperately craving something with vitamin c in it. You creep closer, avoiding loose rocks and trying not to slide as you descend the mountain.

You spy on them and sadly, this becomes a daily habit. They appear to have become lovers and often show affection to each other as they breakfast on their patio. The First Mate has taken to calling

himself "The Baron" and struts up-and-down in
the garden, referring to it as "The Estate." He calls
the Skipper, "The Baroness" and provokes her to
fits of laughter with his posturing. You feel pangs
of loneliness, resentment, and hunger. One day, the
Baron spots you attempting to steal a carrot from
the estate. He laughs and tells the Baroness that he
has spotted "the Skinny Weasel" and they throw
stones at you, driving you away to the safety of the
mountain. You did not get the carrot and you begin
to seethe with hatred for the Baron.

You return to your cave, where you have been
making marks on the wall since your second night
on the island. By your calculations, tonight is
Christmas Eve. You could not even have a carrot
for Christmas, even though the Baron has more
than he can eat. You succumb to tears, once again,
but then you find a hidden source of strength and
stop your tears. You slowly rise to your feet and

shake your fist at the world. You will not be beaten! There must be a way to crush this stupid Baron!

You do have the higher ground. You could find the right spot and encourage the Baron and Baroness to attack you and then set a boulder in motion that would crush them or sweep them from the mountain. They would be dead and you would be left in peace, plus you would have the estate. Are you a homicidal maniac? No, your situation has necessitated different rules than the ones you followed in your suburban life. Once you and the Baron were allies and now you are mortal enemies – that's just how life goes. You decide to keep watching them and pondering your opportunity.

One morning, you are surprised to find that the Baron is 100 feet below you, oblivious to your presence, trying to dig out roots of plants that he wants to move to his estate. There is a rock the size of a large coconut near you… What do you do? Do you call out to him and ask if you guys can discuss a treaty? Do you hurl the rock, fatally wounding the Baron while you have the chance? What if you miss? If you take too long to ponder the dilemma, he will look up to see you and laugh grimly, shouting up to you that you, "Should have done it – that was your one and only chance." What do you do?

This thought experiment illustrates the exact situation that you are in with your fellow high potential coworkers. They want you to be gone and you want them to be gone. Very soon, if not already, you will reveal your enmity and they will make their own moves against you, whether in retaliation or in a pre-emptive strike. This is all as it should be and perfectly natural. It is actually a relief when you can drop your masks with each other. Of course, you have to keep those masks of friendly cooperation firmly in place when managers are around, but otherwise, yes, you can drop the mask and let your face breathe a bit.

Thought Experiment – Poison Darts and a Memo

So the island turns out to be inhabited! The natives were just wisely keeping hidden and observing the atavistic intruders. The indigenous inhabitants, the "Tav Nies" saw all the brutality of the first night and decided that you were the only intruder worth getting to know, but even you were only trusted after long observation.

They approach you slowly, first offering you food, which you desperately need, and then slowly beginning to hang around your cave and even letting their lovely children tease you by pulling your hair and tying you up while you sleep. You find the Tav Nies to be a beautiful, peaceful, friendly people and you feel that you could stay with them forever. They are also smart and funny and sexy, since this is a thought experiment and there is no need to be dull.

The natives get tired of bringing you roasted birds to eat and so they teach you to use their poison dart blowguns. You practice for hours on end with the blowgun and you finally decide that you can probably kill your enemies if the need ever arises, especially if you can get a shot at them while remaining hidden. You learn the Tav Nies language and tell them the whole story of waking up in the night and discovering the horrible plans of the crew. They think it's funny, and ask you to retell it at every fireside dance. You gradually learn the funny part seems to be when you wake up and first realize that they are going to kill you, so you begin to 'ham-up' that part, with big eyes, shudders, gasps, and weeping.

The comedy seems to be that this peaceful tribe never takes human life and thinks that someone who would do such a thing must be a demon. They think it is ridiculous that you ever thought you could escape from supernatural evil beings. You also look funny when you are scared. You have a terrible time convincing them that these are just regular humans. But I digress.

You become great friends with the chief of the Tav Nies and he teaches you many things about surviving on the island. In exchange, he wants you to tell him stories about modern life in the rest of the world. You become fond of your breakfast chats, punctuated by his big, booming laugh, and enlivened by his endless curiosity.

One day, the chief tells you that the old villainous pair of crewmembers has built something like a giant catapult, that shoots large, flaming arrows and that they are wheeling it toward the village, which they have apparently discovered. The chief estimates that murder and pillaging is about to occur. Since the Tav Nies do not kill people and do not really know how, do you mind killing these two nasty characters?

Oh well, you sigh, "I guess in that case, I could go ahead and take my old trusty blowgun and go see what I can do with these nasties. It was going to come down to 'kill or be killed' sooner or later. " Of course it was, what took you so long?

THE POISON DART MEMO

In that classic book of business philosophy, *"The Master Manager,"* I provide many sample memos for you to use to intimidate, manipulate, and terrorize your employees. Many of you find this very helpful and so I will offer one here,

specifically designed for the emerging leader, not

yet a manager. I should not have to warn you not

to use this indiscriminately and to only use it once,

but I will do so in a spirit of wild generosity.

MEMO #3496.2 – NEW PROCEDURE

To: (Colleagues with no power)
From: (Your name)
CC: (People you want to impress)
Re: New Procedure Guidelines

Effective immediately, all systems, tools,

and processes that you utilize in your daily work

must be added to our company inventory. See

attached template for your use. THIS IS DUE BY

JUNE 30. Also attached are guidelines for how to

complete this task. If you feel that your department

should be excluded from this exercise, due to the

exceptions on the attached list, YOU MUST

CONTACT ME TO REGISTER YOUR APPEAL NO

LATER THAN COB TOMORROW. Acceptable

methods of submitting an appeal are outlined in

the procedures documentation. NO TEMPLATES SHOULD BE SUBMITTED AS TEMPLATES. If you need assistance in converting your template to a non-template, review the guidelines. **ALL TEMPLATES MUST BE SUBMITTED NO LATER THAN COB TOMORROW – THERE ARE NO EXCEPTIONS.** Thank you for your participation in this important enterprise-wide initiative! -END OF MEMO

You may be reading this and thinking, "It contains completely contradictory instructions; it is confusing; it is unprofessional in tone; and it will destroy my career." All of this is true, except for the last part.

When you send this genius memo, the people on the "to" line – those with no political power, will read it and instantly hate you, assuming they don't already. The people copied on the memo – the ones that you want to impress, will immediately think that you have more power to disrupt peace and tranquility than they had heretofore guessed. They will read it and re-read it and feel sure that it makes no sense, but will want to get someone else's opinion before replying to all recipients and asking what this memo means.

All recipients will be shaking their heads and muttering about, "One more stupid initiative when there is so much actual work to do." All of this is going to get you noticed, get your name bandied about, get managers to see you as a potential force for disruption, and make your former peers see you as someone who is one a different track, someone who is somehow superior.

What about the firestorm that you have started? Once people start contacting you to ask what this is about, tell them, with the exception of one other "emerging leader" peer, that the memo was "sent in error" and that the "committee will reconvene and draft another memo, but this time there will be better communication prior to rollout."

Be humble, but humorous. These things happen, after all. Keep a laugh in your voice; it is helpful to raise your eyebrows, smile, and shake your head in amazement at the vagaries of life while you are talking, even if you are on the telephone. Your audience will feel the emotion through you voice.

The callers will be relieved that the work has evaporated and they will move on, but the RESIDUAL effect for you will be significant. You have shown that you can disturb the surface of the little pond in which you all live.

What about the one peer who did not get the 'sent in error" message? You must treat this budding leader in a very harsh and high-handed manner. Angrily point out that the memo was clear and contained all that they needed to know, if they would only read it carefully. Lose your temper a bit, but do not use profanity or call them names. (You cannot win if you are fired).

Be sarcastic, angry, abrupt, and remind them repeatedly that you do not have time to keep repeating yourself. What is all this for? That employee will complain about you to his/her manager, co-workers and all who will listen, but no one else will have the same experience.

People will begin to wonder if the complaining employee is really high potential after all. They do not seem to be able to get along with someone so reasonable and easy-going as yourself.

Someone just got a poison dart in the back of the neck … pfffttt.

Conspiracies Digression

The Madhouse

There is an ongoing government experiment that secretly replaces many of the employees of certain companies with people diagnosed as, "persecutory delusional." Management is then salted with people diagnosed as psychopathic and the resulting chaos and loathing is studied for practical applications. This will look much like your own company, so it may be hard to tell if this is happening where you work. If you are part of that experiment, please follow the instructions of the researchers, rather than this book.

The Giant Zipper

There is a 3-mile long zipper in the Arizona desert. It is of unknown origin. The metal of which it is made is unknown to humans. The zipper is 4 feet wide and is guarded 24/7 by elite national security forces. The zipper has never been opened more than 26 inches, but was tested and probed extensively upon its discovery in 1972. Tests were inconclusive, but there was sufficient reason to keep from opening it further. While the above is factual, the following is just my opinion: they probably found that the zipper was keeping the Earth's crust together and that unzipping it would cause the crust of the earth to fall off into space.

Half the World Robots

There is ample reason to believe that, since 1968, over half of the world has consisted of automatons, appearing completely human and behaving in a lifelike manner. The current news about clumsy attempts to make robots that can open refrigerators without ripping off the handles is a subterfuge. Also fake are the photos of college students making clunky androids that look like vacuum cleaners and winning awards when the device can put a ball in a bucket. This is insulting our intelligence, it is so exaggerated. Skin like human skin that feels warm to the touch and can be bruised is 60-year old technology. Even decades ago, robots could be created that sang and danced and fell in love. Now, all of a sudden, all we can make are big, clumsy, tinmen that walk into walls? It is laughable.

The Restroom Fingerprint Plan

Most restroom door handles contain fingerprint sensors. The government is tracking many of your movements. That is why public restrooms and the restrooms in your workplace have handles, when they could easily have foot-pressure activated step-plates that would eliminate the transfer of germs that occurs with all of this "handle grabbing." Big Brother knows every time you go to the bathroom. Many restrooms allow people to push the door to exit without touching the metal plate when they leave. This is because they do not really need your departure time – it is just a "nice to have" so they gather this data haphazardly. They really care about how often you go, not how long you stay. Why do they want to know? They are studying the feasibility of paying people to reduce restroom trips to one per day, through borderline dehydration. The theory is that we can eliminate global warming and water shortages, while saving massive amounts of time if we can stop all this restroom business. Further, the theory is that the average trip to the restroom costs the world the equivalent of $3, while people would be willing to skip going to the restroom for an hour for $2. Over the course of a regular 8-hour day, people could earn $16 and save the world $8. Everybody wins; except that you suffer all the

effects of dehydration and risk various other forms
of physical and psychological damage from all this
restraint. Breaking eggs to bake cakes, I guess.

Regular Communication with Aliens

Planet Earth has been communicating with
aliens since 1994. First it was a top secret global
security initiative, so I understood why the general
public did not get to know about this, but now it is
getting a bit silly; we can certainly handle the truth;
there will not be mass panic. The United Nations
calls-up their alien counterparts and chats on a
weekly call. These aliens are more advanced than
we are, so they get a bit bored with the
conversations, but they are happy to give us useful
advice, since they are 21 billion years older than we
are, as a civilization. They laugh (in their squeaky,
giant insect-like way) when we tell them about our
fuel-shortage worries. They say we can get all the
energy we want from thought-projection and that
we will learn more if we figure it out for ourselves.
The UN generals and commanders find the aliens

rather annoying and egotistical, but defer to them on points of technology and innovation, especially when they levitate in lotus position while sneering at us.

Many People Dead without Knowing

Many humans walking among us today are not robots, but actually dead. An experiment at some of the major teaching hospitals was testing the ability to resuscitate people who were dead for at least 24 hours. The corpses were resuscitated and released into the city. Their brainwaves are still reflective of a dead person, however. The original plan was to install GPS location devices subcutaneously, then occasionally round up the walking dead and bring them back for study updates, but the location devices itched and the "zombies" scratched at them until they fell out. The study fellows have secretly admitted that they no longer know who is dead. "The focus was on the technology working, not really on the numbers."

Mission and Vision … as Weapons

You may be wondering whether it is important for the High Potential Employee to memorize the company vision statement and mission statement. Sadly, yes, even though they are confusing and devoid of meaning. I know; 99% of employees do not know the difference between the two statements. This is the fault of those business schools and business book authors who propagate these ridiculously similar terms. Why are they both called "statements?" Why is anyone surprised that the terms are confused, if the terms are confusing? "Mission Statements" could have been called something with some punch, like "Mission Manifesto" or it could be in plain English, like, "Reason We Exist."

The cheesy-sounding "vision statement" should be called simply, "Future State" or "Ride in Our Time Machine, Baby." See how easy it is to distinguish these two now? Sadly, all the studies that show that companies with clearly-defined mission and vision statements are more successful than those without are false. This is the old "correlation equals causation" fallacy. The companies that these business schools studied do better than average because they are generally paying more attention to all aspects of company guidance and brainwashing than the not-as-successful companies. The success is not from the various statements, but rather the statements and the success are both from the active engagement of executive leadership, who are actively engaged because they are getting paid well, because the company is doing well. Yes, it is circular: Some success leads to the ability to attract and retain better managers, which leads to more success. Don't think too much about it.

The point here is that you should know enough about the mission and vision to articulate them if cornered, but this is secondary to how you can use them to your advantage. What all people on the right side of the singularity know is that mission and vision statements, along with all other company brainwashing tactics, are simply tools with which to browbeat your competition and remove them from the contest. The proper use of these tools can result in a one-punch death blow. Imagine that you are in a meeting with another few HPEs and some Gatekeepers. One of the HPEs is proposing and explaining an idea to cut costs or increase revenue. You should be focusing on one thing only: How can you decisively show that the idea is a violation of the mission or vision?

Do not tell me that this is not always possible –
it is <u>always</u> possible, given the flexibility of
language and the fact that most people cannot
process sudden attacks in time to defend
themselves. Self-defense experts will tell you that
the first punch is more than half the fight, even if
the attacker is physically inferior to the defender.
Our brains cannot immediately process being
attacked out of nowhere by a seemingly harmless
person. By the time we realize we are in a fight, our
capacity is diminishing from the hail of blows
raining down on us. It is exactly the same in
business; no need to actually punch someone in the
face, so stop clenching your fist.

I am going to test my hypothesis by inventing
a random idea to cut cost and then a random
mission statement. I will attempt to show where
the former is a blatant disregard of the latter.

Cost Cutting Idea:

I think we should look at our expense approval process. Currently, the employee who incurred the expense must complete an expense voucher, which goes to their manager, who approves it, then sends it to accounts payable for reimbursement to the employee. The manager is notified when the voucher is awaiting manager approval, and the employee is notified when the voucher is approved. Accounts Payable is notified when a voucher has been approved, and the employee is notified when the expense has been reimbursed. The notifications are automated, so no one has deemed that to be an expense, but the thing that everyone is missing is that each notification takes some time to read.

If we take all that time, annualized, across the entire company, we have many wasted hours of work time. Does the employee really need to know that the manager has approved the expense? Do they really need to know that Accounting has paid the expense? The money will be in their account when it is paid – what else is there to know? Does Accounting really need to know that there is an expense waiting for processing? Why don't they just have a queue that contains what needs to be done?

While this is being proposed, you should be ignoring the question of whether it saves money or adds value at all. Your only focus should be how it can be shown to be a blatant, even aggressive, disregard of your beloved mission statement.

Mission Statement

"We will produce the highest quality widgets backed by the best customer service, in the world."

Your Rebuttal

(You are seething with anger when you finally speak, but start off slowly, to reduce defense tactics). "I'm sorry, but I don't agree. This cutting of corners to save a few pennies may seem like a good idea, but it shows absolute disregard for our mission. How can we produce the highest quality widgets, backed by the best customer service, when we are confusing our employees about something as basic as timely expense reimbursement?"

You make fierce eye contact with each person at the table. There is a lump in your throat.

"Are you actually suggesting that we have employees walking around the building, asking their manager if they received the reimbursement request, asking Accounting if the request is in process, checking their bank account twenty times a day to see if it has posted the reimbursement? Are you *kidding*?"

See that? Feel it? This idea is dead. I don't care how good it was – it's dead and you know it. These were, as promised, totally random ideas and mission statements. It has UNIVERSAL APPLICABILITY. Don't trip over your chair as you leap up and run down the hallway to put this into practice.

"But" you say, "I will be universally hated. I will have no friends. I will be the company pariah." Call a friend and tell them you love them, wipe your tears, and then return to this book.

First, let's clear-up the "friend" concept. This is the workplace. Anyone who uses the term "friend" or acts as if they are more than a temporary ally is manipulating you. There are no friends in business. Don't worry; you don't need them to be happy, just like you don't have to believe in the tooth fairy to be happy. Here is a bonus thought experiment: You are fired tomorrow and get a job as a door-greeter in a large department store. Your "friends" from work stop by the department store on their lunch break, to buy some party supplies. They see you welcoming them to the store. They are obviously surprised to see the change in your fortunes. Do they rush up to you and embrace you and invite you to lunch? Do they plan a lunch that you can attend, given your rigid schedule? Alternatively, do they make lame conversation about, "So how is everything?" "So how's it going?" "So … good to see you…" and then wander off, never to be seen again? I won't put too fine a point on it.

As far as being universally hated, that is just silly. No one at work loves you, so no one at work will hate you – these are excessive emotions that do not pertain to work. Maybe it is time for another **Thought Experiment.**

Thought Experiment – the Treasure Chest

One day on your tropical island, you trap the Baron. You find him in a pit that he fell into and you have a clear shot at him with the blowgun. He absolutely deserves to die and you would be much better off knowing he is no longer a threat. Just as you are about to blow the dart, however, he says, "Wait! I have a box of flares that I have cleverly hidden on the island, along with 25 pounds of gold, a mirror, a needle, a compass, a Swiss Army knife, matches, water purification tablets, kerosene, a cook stove, coffee beans, vegetable seeds, and a bottle of aspirin. If you kill me, all of those things will be wasted, but it you let me live, I will take you to where it is hidden and I will never bother you again."

You smirk cynically, knowing that he will kill you at the first opportunity. He smirks cynically in return, suspecting that you will kill him as soon as he reveals the location of the treasure chest. If you get this treasure, assuming it exists, your chance of being rescued increases exponentially, you will be wealthy once rescued, and you will have a better chance of further survival if not rescued. You do recall that the first mate was lugging some metal box when he got into the life raft. You call down to the first mate, "Hey, what about your partner in crime – isn't she going to feel that you cheated her out of her part of the treasure if you give it to me?" The Baron laughs in his villainous manner. "That weakling doesn't matter. She has been no help at all. In fact, I was planning to kill her off, since she wants to share in the gold." As the Baron was making this despicable little speech, his partner has walked up, unobserved, from the opposite side of the pit from where you are standing.

The Baroness makes a sign for you to be silent and just listens intently at the words of her mate, her frown deepening all the while. Finally, she discloses her presence by saying, "Thanks Darling! It is good to know your true opinion of me." She then turns to you and says, "Since he is in the hole, and you and I are free to move around, and I know where he hid the treasure, please feel free to dart him at any time – we don't need him anymore." The Baron calls up to you, "Do not believe her! I never told her where the treasure is hidden. She is going to get you to trust her and then kill you, then come back and torture me for the treasure location. Think about it! Who told you about the treasure?

Me! Who did she say hid the treasure? Even *she* said it was me. If you have to kill one of us, just to manage us better, shouldn't it be *her*?" Not very romantic now, are they?

Have you noticed that your potential allies and enemies are changing very rapidly? Do you see any value in the term "friend" here? Welcome to the working world. What will you do though? Who should you ally yourself with?

Thought Experiment – Your New Business

So why is the working world this way? I do not like to encourage existential questioning, but I know that many readers will feel that there must be a better way – that we must somehow fight for a better corporate world. Sure, fine, let's look at why it is like it is – I am here to help, after all. The truth is that everyone is not nearly as good as they could be, once they are assimilated into the corporate structure. This is a formula; let Π represent individual human potential and let Σ represent the process of assimilation of the individual into the corporation, which will, necessarily be some value less than 1, and let Ω represent the resulting quality of the worker and thus the corporation. $(\Pi)\Sigma = \Omega$. Elegant, isn't it? Allow me to explain why this is so, with a return to our beautiful little island.

Now that the Tav Nies have befriended you and survival is no longer your constant project, you look for something useful to do. One day you make some paints out of various ground-up minerals. You make a brush from available materials, and you paint yourself a nice seascape visible from just outside your mountain retreat. The painting is on the inside of some tree bark and it seems durable enough to hang by your door.

You are surprised to find that the Tav Nies are delighted and fascinated with your painting. The chief wants to trade gold for your painting, but you owe him your very life and so insist on making a gift of the painting. The next day, you have more visitors bringing gold, asking for paintings. A boy of about ten or eleven years, whom they seem to call "Chippy" starts hanging around, telling you that the two of you could become fabulously wealthy if you go into business together. He is funny and enthusiastic and convinces you to paint two more seascapes. These new paintings sell fast and now Chippy starts helping you make paint, gather bark, clean brushes and so forth. He tells you that, with one more painter, your business could be huge. He has a sister ...

1. The Law of Hopeless Talent Selection

Corporations want people whose knowledge, skills, and abilities fit the needs of the company. This is done by comparing job descriptions with resumes and interviews. Resumes are self-report, so they are useless. Interviews are rarely indicative of actual ability, since they are not the work itself, but a gauge of ability to do the work.

So a partially-quantified job is compared to a qualitative assessment of a candidate. This is obviously hopeless, so most companies just take who they have hired and try to shoehorn them into the jobs that are open.

How are you going to select the right assistant for your art business? You ponder it for a minute, then tell Chippy to bring his sister.

2. **The Law of the Lowest Common Denominator.**

Corporations being groups of people, they make most operational and policy decisions by getting people in a room and looking for agreement. If someone is above average in intelligence and creativity, then the average person will not understand them, so their ideas will never be the lowest common denominator – by definition. How can you be

both 'ahead of your time' and understood by
your time?

Chippy tries to tell you that you should
diversify, but you say that this would risk
losing your appeal and killing the business.
You don't even know if you can paint anything
besides seascapes, plus, why tamper with
success? The new employee, "Janny" is on your
side. She is an elegant and beautiful young
woman who projects a strong self-confidence.
She tells Chippy that he gets carried away
sometimes and goes too far, and this is just such
a case. He tries to explain that market
saturation is fast approaching, but you don't
know what he is talking about, so you and
Janny tell him to go dig up some more red dirt
to make paint with.

3.   The Law of Error Avoidance.

The third law of the reduction of quality is that the pain of being wrong is double the joy of being right. This is, for once, not just my randomly-stated opinion, but an actually phenomenon, carefully researched and demonstrated by controlled experiments. This means that, over time, one is going to become more and more hesitant to posit an idea – the downside is double the upside – so why should you? Add to that the tendency for colleagues and management to exploit anything perceived as a blunder in order to advance their own pitiful reputations. If you are playing defense all the time, you cannot do much on offense, now can you? Companies can only overcome this tendency if they reduce the stigma for being wrong and increase the reward for being right. Some truly great companies reward both wrong and right, as long as a person is contributing ideas. These companies are anomalies and threaten to destabilize the entire universe.

The chief has been like a board of
directors for your budding company, guiding and
advising you as you have grown. You awake
unusually early one morning and go down to the
beach to walk and see the sunrise. You get a great
idea! You will rent your pictures to those who do
not have enough gold to buy one outright. Once
they have paid roughly 150% of the original cost,
they will own the painting. You return to the cave
and, after breakfast, gather the Chief, Chippy, and
Janny in the cave boardroom and your excitedly
present your idea. As you elaborate on your idea,
Janny and Chippy look at each other and frown
and the Chief breaks into raucous laughter. When
the Chief finally stops laughing and wipes the tears
from his eyes, he tells you that no one on the island
ever rents anything; that the concept is absurd. You
feel a bit foolish. You ask Janny and Chippy what
they think and they both ask why anyone would
want to have something in their possession that is
not actually theirs, then eventually pay more to

finally own it. They seem embarrassed on your behalf. You feel miserable. You lamely state that good ideas only come after some bad ideas, but Chippy asks you what bad ideas preceded your good idea of the initial painting. You secretly resolve to take no more sunrise walks on the beach.

4. The Law of Measurement Stupidity

Industrial engineering is generally a good thing. Things like changing the layout of a factory floor to allow production to flow better are straightforward in their implementation and value. How many tons of coal have been extracted from a mine is obviously an important measure for a coal mining business. Measurement also lends legitimacy, justifies employment and other types of expenditure, and gives management a sense of control over the destiny of their business.

The stupidity comes in when
corporations try to measure things that are:

1. Worth measuring, but not measurable,

2. Measurable, but not worth measuring, or

3. Neither measurable nor worth measuring.

For example, the number of hours an office
employee <u>works</u> per day is worth measuring, but
not measurable. The number of hours that the
employee is <u>in the workplace</u> is measurable, but
not worth measuring. Companies measure it
anyway, because it gives them a sense of control
over the employee. Time-in-chair is not equal to
valuable output.

The result is that employees drag uncreative
minds inside exhausted bodies into the workplace
and flop into their desk chairs, vegetate for a few
minutes, then sigh and haul themselves to the
coffeepot to get enough caffeine to stay awake. This

satisfies the measured requirement, so it is what gets done.

Imagine if a company told its employees, "Work as many or as few hours as you want to, but you must reduce costs or increase revenue equal to your salary each year to remain employed." This is impossible. Companies will not do it because workers are not accustomed to such requirements and would leave the company as quickly as possible.

Other useless things are unofficially measured: Punctuality to meetings, attendance at company events, wardrobe, political connections, friendliness, participation in fundraisers, and physical attractiveness.

You finally realized that you should be paying Janny and Chippy for their work. You give them both a tiny piece of gold for their past three weeks of work. They stare at the dot in the palm of their hand with confused expressions. They look at each other, then back to the pay, then back to your face. Chippy says not to worry – that they are just happy to work with you and be part of something interesting. Janny nods lamely. They seem a bit crestfallen. You do not like this negative vibe, so you look puzzled as well and say, "Oh, I almost forgot," and give them both another small nugget. The atmosphere has not improved much, so you go back to painting and Chippy and Janny go for a walk.

That evening, you draft a schedule, list of duties, and generous pay plan for your staff. You resolve to review it with the Chief and then present it to your team. The next morning, you miss seeing Chippy and Janny bounding into the cave, Chippy chattering away about his plans, and Janny smiling at him indulgently. Chippy and Janny finally walk into the cave at mid-morning with long faces and slow steps. You begin to wonder if this is going to be a regular thing. If that is so, maybe you will be overpaying them at this point? You decide to start recording their arrival and departure times. They notice you looking at your watch and scribbling in your journal. They exchange dark looks.

5. The Law of Inverse Intelligence to Power

Bees, ants, ravens, and possibly other non-human animals can engage in linguistic displacement, i.e., communicate with their community about things that are not *here*, or are not here *now*. For example, a bee performing a dance to tell the others where nectar can be found, is displacement, since the thing to which it refers is not present for the other bees. Humans were once thought to be the only animals with this ability, but this is not so. As managers gain power, their ability to engage in linguistic displacement deteriorates in equal measure. Soon they can only talk about what is in front of them, or happening right now, or both. The problem with that is that management should be setting goals, identifying steps to reach those goals, and using company resources to execute those steps. That type of thinking, let's call it "strategic," is not immediate, temporally or spatially, so it requires displacement. Not only do managers lose the ability to talk to you about things not temporally or spatially present, but they also lose the ability to understand when you discuss such things. All displaced communication to them will sound like a waterfall, a buzzing fly, or heavy rain. In desperation, the manager will complement your watch, or your pen, or ask you a question that has no importance to them, such as how your family is doing these days. All this time, you thought you were boring your manager by offering suggestions for long-term company improvements, but no, your manager never heard the actual words.

How does the "law of inverse intelligence" actually operate? "Working memory" is the short-term memory that holds information about a conversation long enough to stay on-topic. Working memory has a limited capacity and items in that memory compete for space. Managers are already using most of their working memory to hold items related to staying in power, including manipulating you and, as subsets of that, intimidating or corrupting you. To engage in linguistic displacement, the manager would need a sizable portion of their working memory to be available, so that they could analyze and respond to your input. Since this capacity is not available, managers are not storing what you are trying to convey. As a survival mechanism, their brain reduces the superfluous input to white noise, thereby keeping it out of competition for space. Imagine how disorienting it would be if the manager did not do this, but allowed your input to enter their working memory! The manager would suddenly recall, with horror, that they had stopped holding the fundamental survival tactics in their memory. This recollection of their mission would come from the limbic part of the brain, the last thing they will ever lose.

Janny and Chippy ask you for a meeting in the cave boardroom. They seem excited, which is a nice change. Brilliant smiles flash, eyes shine, laughter is heard. You go into the room with them and they begin to describe a plan to paint a massive mural on the outside cave wall. Your mind drifts … why are they talking about doing something that does not pay? Don't you have enough to do already? Do they think you are a machine? Janny babbles on about the attention that this would generate, about the children of the tribe coming to watch you and to learn about painting. Chippy jumps out of his chair and begins dancing around the room, talking about how he and his friends could help. You think about how much gold you have saved – probably $100,000 worth, if gold is the same price per ounce as when you sailed… Is the gold safe? Should you move your hiding place? Have the kids ever noticed where you hid it? Janny and Chippy are watching you as if they have asked you a question that you have failed to notice. You decide it is time to wrap-up the meeting.

So these immutable laws of nature are the reasons that workers and corporations will never be good as they could be and workers will contribute a fraction of what they could. This makes companies a fraction of what they could be and, in turn makes the world a fraction of what it might have been. $(\Pi)\Sigma = \Omega$.

Thought Experiment – the Guru

So even though I have provided you with the
"Weasely Rationalizations Toolkit" (see Appendix
A), you still think that the tactics outlined in this
book are morally suspect. With this in mind, we
have provided another thought experiment, this
time a conversation with a Zen Buddhist Yogi kind
of guy, known for his perfect moral compass and
great wisdom. He lives in a cave on the top of a
mountain, sipping tea and meditating. He wears a
tattered robe and woven sandals. His beard is long
and white and his head is shaved. The guru

radiates health and goodwill, his skin glowing and his eyes gleaming with intelligence and humor. Watch how I **run circles around him** – it's pitiful, but necessary.

Me: Thank you for letting me invade your mountain retreat Guru, I promise it will be worth your while.

G: (Laughing) I am sure it will be. Would you like some hot green tea?

Me: Yes please. Now Guru, let's get down to business; this mountain wind is chilling me and this cave is not exactly cozy.

G: We are actually in a Starbucks.

Me: This is my thought experiment and I can locate it wherever I want to. I can put us on a meteor if I so choose.

G: Fair enough.

Me: The message that I sent you explained that I am writing a business book and that I want you to review it and tell me if it is a good and wise book.

G: I have reviewed your manuscript. It is amusing, but I would not call it wise or good. You will ask me why I say so. Your book presupposes that the reader's sole object is to achieve a secure and highly-paid position in the corporate world. Further, you assume that the only way to attain such success is through the ruthless and paranoid destruction of other people's success – a zero-sum game, in other words. Both assumptions are erroneous.

Me: You are wrong on both counts, Guru. First, the assumption that people buy my book because they want to achieve success in the corporate world is a sound one, given the title of the book and the excerpt on the back of the book. Whether that is their "sole object or not" is unknowable. I would guess they have other goals in life, but that is not my problem. They can benefit from the book, even if success is just one of their objectives.

G: If the achievement of that one objective is at the expense of their other objectives, then the book has not served them well. You did not answer the second point.

Me: I am getting there, Guru. My response to your second point is that my way is the only way, which I guess you do not agree with.

G: No, I do not agree. In fact, you have offered no evidence to the reader that your methods are effective, even if the reader did want to adopt such tactics. All of this, "Kick everyone off the boat and kill your enemies" is actually short-sighted and leads to both failure and unhappiness.

Me: Oh you know that, do you? I have read your biography and I do not recall that you are the retired CEO of an international conglomerate who made his fortune by thirty years of age and retired to this mountaintop to meditate. In fact, I think your father was a merchant and struggled to pay your way through school.

G: Yes, my origins are humble, as are my current circumstances. You knew that before you climbed this mountain to speak with me, yet you requested a meeting and you came. I can only assume that you want to hear what I have to say.

Me: Oh yes, yes. I respect your reputation very much. Please do tell me what you think.

G: Ok, I will. I think you are throwing nets at the feet of your fellow humans, tripping and ensnaring them with your terrible advice.

Me: That's pretty strong talk Guru – I don't know why I asked you. If you valued money and success, you would not be sitting up on this rock, dressed in tattered robes, drinking tea from a chipped teapot, would you?

G: (Laughing) Exactly so! Money and your version of success are nothing to me. When you were a child, you begged your parents to take you to theme parks and circuses, to stop at roadside tourist shops, where you would dream of buying plastic toys. You now could do all those things, but you do not, because you see them as trivial. Consider that there may be people who see your current interests as trivial. As a child, you could not have imagined that someone would not want a triple scoop of chocolate ice cream every day. Today, you cannot imagine that anyone would *not* want to be wealthy and important. Yet it is so.

Me: I will have to take your word for it, since you admit that I cannot imagine it. I am advising people on how to get what they want from life before it's over; how to get their little bit of happiness to partially compensate for all the trouble and grief of life. Is that so bad?

G: On the contrary, you are helping to blind people to the fact that they have everything they need to be happy – they have always had it and they always will. There is no need to 'get' something – there is only a need to understand. Suffering comes from desire.

Attraction and aversion are the source of suffering, not existence itself.

Me: I just don't agree with you. You are only chilled-out up here because you already have gotten the things that you want and now you are ready to relax. Am I right?

G: You are correct in thinking that I already have what I want, because I want nothing. You think that activities that feed your ego are somehow a compensation for the brevity of life, yet you know that your ego will die along with your body. In fact, you will forget most of your acquisition and conquest before you even die.

Me: I am raging against death and nothingness. I am doing something to combat the nothingness.

G: There are two kinds of emptiness: emptiness from vanity and emptiness that is full; outside of time and space. Embrace the emptiness that is full and you will not fear the void.

[Here the guru pours some more tea for me and sips from his own cup]

G: You and I are not so different. We both think that everything matters and nothing matters. For example, I have taken great care in preparing and presenting this tea to you – as if it were the most important thing in the world ... yet it would not bother me if all tea and teapots in the world disappeared. You seem to place great importance on success in the corporate world, yet you know you are not doing anything that matters – you are sarcastic about it all.

Me: (Laughing) Forgive my sarcasm then. Dostoevsky said, "Sarcasm is the last refuge of modest people when the privacy of their soul is invaded." But perhaps you are right guru, nothing matters and everything matters at the same time. If tea is so important to you though, why do you have an ugly old chipped teapot?

G: On the contrary, I looked far and wide for a chipped teapot – that is just *wabi-sabi*.

Me: Just what?

G: Wabi-sabi. Look it up.

Me: Sure, ok, I think it is some sort of Asian horseradish – very hot! Thanks for the tea Guru. I hope you learned something today!

G: Oh yes, I did - thank you and goodbye!

APPENDIX:

The Weasely Rationalizations Toolkit

You are doing all these sneaky things to make more money. You will give 10% of your money to charities that feed starving children, so the most moral thing for you to do is to make the most money possible. You are only eliminating fellow weasels, who will just find another job somewhere else; meanwhile you are saving children's lives!

By getting rid of other people just like you from the workplace, you are actually reducing the total number of nasty people in your company, consolidating them down to just a few, such as yourself, and you are not so bad.

Anyway, in a dog-eat-dog world, becoming food for another dog serves no purpose except to make that other dog stronger, so he can eat more dogs. So better to be the eater, so you can eat the really bad dog and prevent some bad things from happening.

In any case, what is "good" and what is "bad?" Such dualistic thinking is naïve; it only allows people to manipulate those who wish to be "good" due to some vestige of their childhood socialization. There is no such thing as "good" – there is only what the majority decides is in their best interest at the moment. Why should you participate in that groupthink? 'Good' is what is best for you.

BOOK 3: The Master Manager

BY STEPHEN MCLOUGHLIN

Contents

ACKNOWLEDGMENTS

Thank you Essie, Billy, Nigel, Ella, and Teya

The Cure

This book is a hot pill of lead for executives. If you can manage to swallow it – you will be cured of all the stupid business advice you have ingested over your career. Stop devising new strategies every month! The poor workers are terrified: $500,000 managers are wandering around bookstores looking for answers; sneaking dirty little peeks at "CEO for Dummies."

Leaders! Think of the poor beleaguered rank and file! Their fearless leaders don't know from one day to the next whether they're General

Patton, Gandhi, Sun Tzu, Lao Tzu, Kung Fu or Mother Goose.

Are you a "servant leader" or Attila the Hun? It might depend on what book was near you as you sipped coffee and browsed an airport bookshop. Are you going to, "break all the rules" or, "get the right people on the bus?" Are you going to make sure we're all, "rowing together" or send us, "alone to the mountain?" What cube-trapped drone wants to think of the executive team sequestered in the boardroom with their shoes off, chanting success mantras?

NEXT: Let's take a look at how you came to be in such a mess.

You

How did you get this way? You are not to blame. You are busy. So busy you no longer have time to plan, just react. Two vitally important points before we proceed:

1. It is good that you have no time to plan, because if you did have time to plan, you would realize that you have no ideas.

2. It is good that you have no ideas because, if you did, they would be bad ideas.

Why is this so? This is because you have spent too much of your life trying to advance and preserve your position, and not enough time doing actual work. You hold endless meetings and conference calls – to no purpose - they have become ends in themselves. You can't remember when you actually produced anything, because all you do is worry about preserving and enhancing your position. You used to know how to work, that's how you began to advance, but now you only know how to preserve. On top of all that, if you are really important, there is a constant buzz in your head that will drive you insane if you ever slow down enough to hear it. This does not mean you are a bad person! Still, your ideas could hurt people, so if you are not going to read this book, please just go to your golf game a little early when the temptation seizes you to do some work or to have an idea. Everyone will be much better off.

If you tend to say, "I almost think that …" throw this book away – no one can help you. Otherwise, read on, there is still hope!

If you invaded a walled city and conquered it, what would be the first thing you would do? Fix the holes in the walls. What next? Make the walls better than they were when you breached them.

That is all you are doing in your job, preserving what you have gained. Your behavior is completely natural! Smile now.

Since you probably have a five-second attention span and about 30 seconds of memory, you have been struggling to remember what all the other business advice books said. Feel free to forget all that; just "drop the raft at the shore," it has done its work. This book will take over now, and will ask much less of you, so it is already better. Exhale.

This book will not give you scope, purpose, mission, goals, targets, or metrics! You have heard that if you don't measure it, you cannot understand it, and if you don't understand it, you cannot improve it. Crap. As Einstein may have said, not everything measurable should be measured and not everything worth measuring is measurable. If you noticed termites had infested your house, would you measure the size of the holes in the walls? Count the termites? Try to time how long it takes a termite colony to eat a cubic inch of wood? No, you would call an exterminator and say, "Do your thing." Right? So stop measuring already.

Business gurus will teach you to measure the right things in the right way with the right people at the right time for the right reasons with the right incentives for the right results! Feel the energy?

Balderdash. Six Sigma? Do you know why you don't understand it? Because it is unnecessarily hard, that's why. It's just choosing the questions you know you can answer; measuring the measurable and playing statistical games to show how "quantitative" it all is. Come on now. Go put some six sigma on your garden.

Anybody can pick up enough business jargon to write a book claiming to enlighten the aimless executive, but this is no set of trite aphorisms. By the time you finish this book, you will be a new manager and you will know exactly how to lead your company! This will take no effort on your part. Feel it yet?

It may be that business executives have such foggy minds and short attention spans that they can only read short books with one-line quotes in them, but I have faith in you!

(Just in case, maybe the Seven Masterful Rules in the following chapter will hold you for one more minute – please stay; see footnotes for those with longer attention spans).

The Seven Masterful Rules

1. Use the universal "action bias" to your advantage; always make the first move.

2. No one gets fired for not making sense

3. The process is the problem, don't blame people.

4. First on the field controls the action.

5. Preparation is not everything, in fact it is NOTHING

6. Drop leadership and you will become the longed-for leader

7. There are various universes in the multiverse; you don't have to succeed in this particular one.

We hope these rules helped, or kept this book in your hand while your flight left (now you might as well buy it and read it while you wait).

Gaining Control

Step 1: Cut costs

Cutting costs is decisive. As you know, your "top line" is strong and healthy, but your "bottom line" is under pressure. (At least that's what you tell investors). What does this mean? Simply that you sell enough, but you spend too much to do it! The steps below will help you keep more of what you earn. Recall that this book is privileged! Cut and paste the following as a company-wide memo.

SAMPLE MEMO

1. The first thing we are going to implement is "freedom from caffeine month" which will eliminate the wasteful coffee catering service and will evolve into the program, "freedom from caffeine for life." We know that companies provided coffee free to employees in the first place because they thought that this improved productivity, but studies have recently shown that this perceived "busy-ness" is more than offset by the employees becoming more talkative and rebellious. Why should we pay someone to babble on endlessly about what's wrong with pollution or war or some inescapable fact of life?

2. Going forward we will not pay for office supplies. Candidates for employment will be asked at the interview stage if they have the "tools of the trade" that they can bring to the job

if hired. When they ask what these tools are, hiring managers should tell them as professionals, they should carry their own pens, legal pads, notepaper, staplers, etc., and bring those to wherever they practice their trade. If they balk at this, they would never be "top players" anyway. This could result in significant savings for our company and, if the pilot program goes well, we will expand the list to personal computers, fax machines, and even copiers as "tools of the trade."

3. A not-trivial sum of money can be saved by eliminating excessive water use in the restrooms. One need only spend some time hiding in a bathroom stall to note the constant flushing that goes on in our staff bathrooms. We executives are not ones to make reactionary policy decisions from some isolated anecdotal

case as a substitute for true management – so that's not what this is about, but I noticed that one employee flushed the toilet three times in one sitting. I fumed as I sat in my hiding place, thinking of the money that was literally going down the toilet. I devised the following rules at that time:

a. Any employee caught flushing the toilet more than once will be dismissed on the spot. Remember, "Fear is a Magnet" and if you sit in there flushing and afraid, we will feel drawn to come and terminate you.

b. No employee should flush the toilet if someone is waiting to use the same toilet, it will be flushed by the subsequent user. This will be known as the "warm seat" rule.

c. If an employee has not put "anything of substance" in the toilet within one minute, he should leave it as is and go back to work.

Cut Costs with Terminations

To let employees know that they can disappear if they do not cooperate, set an example randomly. Don't be squeamish. By the way, call them anything except employees; call them "team-members" "associates" "partners" "clients" – anything that helps them feel special; it's free. When you do have to fire someone, call it an "opportunity" and announce that this employee has left the company – you announce it with mixed emotions, since she is leaving us, but pursuing a career enhancing opportunity. You know that the rest, "understand and appreciate" the changes that are happening in the company that will make it a better place. See? That was easy. Find a good "angel of death" in Human Resources that can terminate with empathy, respect, and calm. To spot a good 'death angel', look around for who can put on the best long face (think attendee at the funeral of a distant relative) when needed, but laugh with you in private a minute later. Avoid those with pesky consciences and, "do the right thing" nonsense.

Cut Costs with Less Communication

Refrain from sending silly and pointless letters on your vision for the company or how everyone needs to try harder. Never send threatening or "gloom-and-doom memos." If you feel some pent-up aggression, take up rock-climbing or some other such cathartic sport. If you take umbrage when you overhear light-hearted banter about "stupid adverse weather policies" or "those crusty, shuffling, mandarins on the top floor" - that's what you get for eavesdropping.

Step 2: Institute Unusual Policies

If you want to make a name for yourself and your company, there is no shorter route than taking commonplace policies and making them farcical or draconian, or preferably, both. A good place to start is with your adverse weather policy.

Adverse Weather Policy

In the event of adverse weather, please stay home, but generate enough production to warrant your existence. Failure to do so will not result in any punitive measures from your employer, but you will run the risk of spontaneous combustion. If you have not brought any work home and are at a loss for how to be productive, sit down with a legal pad and pen and make your five-year work plan. If only the first quarter of that five-year plan involves working for this particular company, you may dispense with the five-year plan and make paper hearts or angels, but, by all means, please stay productive.

What is there to take offense from in that memo? One cannot help but think, if such creativity would spread to product development, you might not be so worried about your annual report to stockholders!

Step 3: When in doubt, create an ad hoc team (details to follow)

Please recall - well, never mind recalling, I'll repeat myself – this not about reality, and the further you move down the continuum, away from reality, the more successful your "initiatives" will be perceived. For team selection, define the "universe of persons" that you will be utilizing in your project. The team will meet on a regular basis to plan a "strategy for implementation." Even if the problem were truly daunting, for example that we were losing planets on a regular basis , you would still create an ad hoc team, so this is always the first step. Tell everyone to find their name on the project list (to make people feel simultaneously special and worried) and to be prepared to discuss "current status" in full detail at next meeting. See the terror? Everyone will blame themselves for not knowing how to prepare for the meeting, which magnifies your power.

Step 4: Preparation is nothing.

Not being prepared for a meeting or presentation is not a problem, despite what most business books say. Being discovered in your lack of preparation by a superior (if there is one in your world) is disconcerting. That's why I will tell you how to: Never be discovered as unprepared.

Let's say that today is the day of your presentation to the CEO and CFO regarding an important matter. You have wisely not prepared, but you are feeling nervous about the fact – you feel that they actually expect something substantive from you. Easy – just talk about what you know, rather than what they want. Let's take an extreme example: All you know at the moment you stand before them is that you don't like pom-poms on socks. That is all you know in the whole world at that moment. That's a perfectly good place to start! Let's watch:

"Good morning to you both. Going forward, it has been discussed and approved by committee - and I would like to make special mention of my appreciation to the other members of the committee

for their hard work and dedication - that we should be able to wear crew socks with pompoms as long as they do not get that tacky soiled look, which makes a pompom instantly morph from cute to evil. After much group discussion and careful review by our legal team, we have decided to tear a gaping hole in space-time to see if we can climb through it, or at least locate the facsimiles we have sent before 5 p.m. today. I appreciate your leadership and I never forget what I have learned here: The only thing that moves at the speed of light is light itself. (Everything else increases in mass to the point where an infinite amount of energy would be needed to increase the speed). The point of these last two sentences is that we are working at the speed of light to reach our goals."

Feel that? I sense that someone has gained complete control.

Note:

Keep in mind; no one gets fired for not making sense. Read that again. People get fired for not generating enough money, political missteps, gross misconduct, malfeasance, or humility, but no one gets fired for being hard to decipher. Even better, people will think you are brilliant and will be embarrassed to say they did not understand your point. As you advance in your organization, they will become ever more afraid to attack your incoherence. If you apologize for anything, they will hate you, but if you stitch together a bunch of non-sequiturs, they will be in awe. Many nonsensical comments have become standard business parlance. Consider "perception is reality" spoken with force and some irritation – it's stupid, but it works – if perception were reality, there would be no insane asylums. Pause – think that over – it's true. Somewhere, someone threw this on the table to buy time, and it became business lore. Another great one is, "There is no reason why this could not be accomplished." Think about that one. There is no reason why we couldn't see fairies dancing in our coffee cups, if only they would. A proposal should have a positive reason to succeed, not just hinge on "no reason it cannot work." These ridiculous comments and many more can really drive a proposal. Salt the proposal with a few clichés and smile brilliantly and you are nearly there. Fellow executives are squeamish about "stepping on hope," so always be hopeful.

SAMPLE MEMO

Speaking of facsimiles and the inevitable semiotic disasters that occur in our paper communications, no reason has been shown why we cannot send all future communications simply by mind-energy and therefore realize significant cost-savings and reduce paper consumption. I, for one, have heard the thoughts of various members of the vendor team, even though their mouths were not moving. Putting aside the fact that their thoughts were trivial, annoying, and even reprehensible, it was a demonstrably less expensive and quicker method of communication. Next steps will depend on various things, including some clear directions from alien life forms that will hopefully visit us and provide not only upgrades to our outdated communications devices, but also clear instructions in proper procedures. We need to plan ahead for this event and "put up our tent before it is dark." We need to develop a work-plan so that we can, "fix our roof before it rains." There is no better time than right now to implement this project plan and we should obviously, "dig our well before we're thirsty."

Sometimes, despite being hopeful, you need to issue stern warnings, just to show that the old dog still has sharp teeth. Following is a template for a stern warning.

SAMPLE MEMO

Communications using internal email is strictly proscribed. No foreign words or phrases may be utilized. Witty bits of Latin and Greek are strictly prohibited. Any thinly veiled sarcasm will be ferreted out and severely punished. Consider yourself a bon vivant? Better erase such thoughts from your mind. Do you like to make a last-minute joke, right at the end of your email?

Keep it up and we will fire you. Is that funny? Still? We didn't think so.

Note:

Do not worry about appearing as the nice Zen executive. Remember; weak leadership will sink the company ship. If someone is threatening your executive bliss, tomorrow he should be sitting in a plastic chair in the unemployment office, filling out forms. Give him an impossible task, and then send the 'death angel' to whack him.

Here is a sample of a good pre-fire task:

This afternoon, please identify the sources of error in our various processes across the enterprise. You may compile in any manner you wish, but I would suggest a searchable database, with designations for such things as name of source, result, cause, dates of errors, impact (financial and reputational), associates responsible, recommended solution, and time to remedy the problem – but I am just throwing out a suggestion. Once you get the database complete, please email me before COB today. Oh, make sure we can query it and report off it. Any questions, reach me on my mobile.

P.S. I really need this by 5 p.m. – don't fail me.

Note:

Executives must alternate between being humorous and being totally devoid of a sense of humor. This creates fear and uncertainty, which increases power. If I am afraid of your moods and do not how you will react in a given situation, I am your prisoner. Send a memo like the following:

SAMPLE MEMO

You may think that it is a big joke to make a shortcut on your computer desktop that says, "implode computer," but we can assure you that it is not funny at all and will very likely result in an implosion of your computer. Do not test this assertion as it will prove only too true and we will not replace your machine. If you have such a time surplus and excess of creativity, please put it to good use by inventing an annual financial report that can be simultaneously true and profitable. Tip: See our brief discussion of Schrödinger's Cat below and look elsewhere for a description on the thought experiment, "the Quantum Suicide Machine." This should get you started.

Annual Reports

Now that I mention your annual report to stockholders, never say, "We had a lot of bad luck." Why do we distrust someone when they say "lucky?" We distrust them because it is true. Truth is scary and awkward. Sincerity is a sign of pending lunacy. What does "good fortune" convey? If in your annual report, you state that certain fortuitous events occurred which resulted in an anomaly in the profit trend line it sounds markedly better than, "We made money because we got lucky." What about the fact that sometimes, the truth is that you had some bad luck? Just say, "A series of unforeseeable events combined to make for a challenging profit environment in third quarter." You might survive if you say that. I know you won't survive if you say, "Bad luck piled up on us and we could not make any money."

Reading Past the First Line

Executives generally read only the first line of everything; very good executives read the first and last line. I recommend reading only parenthetical statements and footnotes. Notice the collection memo below. This is a real memo that gained kudos for the collections department in a large financial institution for their tough-minded collection letter. Clever and subversive workers know that parentheses are a narcotic for executives and they are used effectively here:

You must respond to this letter within the next five business days. There will be no appeal if you do not respond in time! (This may sound stern, but we do not mean for it to be so. We're actually just two old guys dressed in worn-out cardigans, warming our feet by wheezing old radiators and a decrepit snoring dog. We scare people for no other reason than we want to make them happy later on by writing something like, "You have missed the stated deadline and you may not appeal our decision, but we have forgiven your debt anyway and best wishes to you and yours." This fills us with delight and we never fail to roar with laughter and pound each other on the back when we write such happy lines). There is no appeal to this decision.

Think what their manager could have spotted by reading the parenthetical! This same mischievous collections department pulled the old, "executives won't read more than 20 words" trick in the following form:

To enroll, please complete the form provided. If you do not fully and accurately complete the form provided, you will not only cease to exist, but also the planet that you lived on will cease to exist. We will all cease to exist, but we will be on a new ... okay - this is getting too complicated , we lied, we can't do anything to you at all, but please fill out the form completely.

Note:

Since you are such a busy manager, why waste time couching your "flavor of the month" management theory in terms of how "this time is different"? Confuse your employees with half-truths. Following is a guide.

We read a book that made us realize that we can be open with our "people." Since, "the things we look at change when we change the way we look at things," we are changing the entire planning process for our company. We will imagine the world we want and it will be manifested for us. Everyone in our company wants to support us and give us more money and lifetime appointments. Beginning tomorrow, we will be renaming offices and hallways after our illustrious selves. Simultaneously, we will send company-wide emails that announce our promotions and lifetime appointments. That should be a sufficiently new way to look at things and I imagine that things will change quite rapidly for us. You are afraid that we will be unceremoniously sacked and escorted from the premises? Not to worry my friend! When they open the "box" called "our reality," the universe will split into two separate universes. Just as there will be one containing an observer looking at a box with a dead cat, and one containing an observer looking at a box with a live cat; we will

find ourselves in one universe where we are
disgraced and one where we are wealthy and
powerful.

Conspiracies Digression

I suggest that one way that you can cement
your grip on power and fame is by courageously
revealing the conspiracies that many people have
suspected all along, but no one has dared to
expose. You will be lauded as the next Upton
Sinclair. Here is a sample Conspiracy Expose'
Project that, although it is probably not directly
related to your job description, you can wedge in
between your other duties as a selfless
contribution to your company's future.

Conspiracy Exposé Project

There are many well-known conspiracies that we are too apathetic to protest about. Coffee is laced with cocaine to make people like it more and to be more productive at work. That's why your nose itches when you drink a lot of it. You may ask, why would a company spend all that money on cocaine, just to make us a little more productive? All what money? Cocaine is only expensive because it's against the law to sell it. In fact, you can make cocaine at home by growing a special kind of mold in a dish. Your only expense is the starter, which costs less than a dollar. Companies can make their own in a utility closet and add it to the coffeemaker or contract with the coffee supply companies to put it in when they make the coffee grounds.

One terrible fact is that telephone makers know that telephones harbor parasites in the earpieces that can get in your ears and live off your brain. They don't do much damage, but gradually make your speech slurred. That's why many elderly people have slurred speech – years of work from the phone parasites. Telephone makers had planned to make the earpieces parasite proof, but a special group of pseudo-governmental agents showed them that the country was better off if older people became unintelligible and thus made room for younger workers.

The strings on teabags are made from hemp –another word for marijuana – so that people could smoke all the free pot that they wanted, but the anti-drug movement made sure that arsenic was added to the teabag strings so people would die if they smoked it.

Water filters are recycled! Yes, the filter you use for your water was used hundreds of other times by people all over the world. Some guy in the Midwest used your filter to clean his fish tank before you started religiously filtering your water with it.

Many other conspiracies exist; have you not wondered why so many people die in car accidents? Why don't they make cars out of rubber? Easy – funeral home directors working with ambulance drivers have pressured automakers to "leave this one alone." You may want to leave it alone as well.

Here are a few more "throwaways" that I can give you, just to give you a tiny bit more exposure to the Real World:

1) We are clones! Yes, we are. The world was about to end three years ago and scientists cloned the entire world population to preserve the

world. When the world did not end as expected, we were about to have too many people, so the scientists made a plague that we clones would be immune to, but they "the originals" would not be immune to. They died off and we were born. It was very well done, almost seamless. I only uncovered the facts by a series of logical deductions, too lengthy and complicated for the scope of this paper.

2) There has never been an eclipse of the sun! In fact, the sun moves all over the place and that whole "heliocentric" hoax was uncovered years ago (just suppressed). There has never been an eclipse, because the sun keeps moving and cannot be in shadow. Our forefathers invented eclipses because they were getting old and had cataracts and wanted some way to explain their fuzzy vision while preserving their vanity. In truth, when your teachers tell you that there is an

eclipse coming, you believe you see a shadow, but you are told not to look at the sun – it will damage your eyes! Can you believe that we still fall for such garbage? [Still, don't look at the sun during one of these fake "eclipses" because people who need to perpetuate this myth will be beaming radiation from space to burn your eyes, just to prove their point!]

Bonus Memos

Not yet ready for the conspiracy project? Not to worry, here is a nice solid boring memo that you can send to the CEO (surely you report to the CEO by now or ARE the CEO) any time you have missed work to "attend a conference" and are not sure what to say when you return:

SAMPLE MEMO

I recently had the honor of participating in a conference which featured specific concerned consulting experts and third-party companies.

Employers are concerned about pending legislation to tax 90% of all employer profits. This could obviously have a dampening effect on corporate viability and may well even suppress stock returns. Our company will emerge unscathed from such regressive tactics and this is no concern on that front. We will be watching with great interest to see whether the house and senate bills are reconciled before the next congressional recess.

Beautiful, no? I bet you could use this right now! The next memo template is a little less universal, yet more powerful than the previous samples. Used well, it could take you to the top. Use it if you feel like an "unknown quantity" and think that it's time to make your mark.

SAMPLE MEMO

This is mostly a case of the Bolsheviks being cleverly managed by the mandarins in the corporate office. I am very concerned about employees misquoting snippets of conversation and the contents of leaked, "eyes only" memos. This is how we get to the point where a cartoon is misquoting a literary masterpiece and then someone is quoting what they heard in the cartoon and putting that in a movie, which someone else quotes, thinking that it sounds intellectual, and uses it in a song. They have promulgated such derivative ideas; they have become trapped in a death spiral of reducing quality, which can only end in pornography or impressionism.

Presentations

Presentations make some executives nervous, especially those who have attained their position without merit – hello dear reader – but not to worry. All planned meetings and presentations are, by definition, a complete waste of time. Furthermore, the trend is to communicate the "presentation qua presentation" rather than actually presenting, so you can anesthetize all the attendee's brains by telling them format items until they can no longer hear. No matter the subject, you can use the following template:

It is a great pleasure to present to you today. Our gratitude goes to the organizers of this meeting. We will begin by introducing the members of our team and launch right into our presentation by giving a general overview of the topic. Please see the outline for the specific sub-topics of our presentation. The body of our presentation will cover the major points of subject matter and will segue into our summary of points covered. There will be a brief question-and-answer period, at which time we will field questions from the attendees. At the conclusion of the presentation, we will end with concluding remarks. We have a lot of material to cover, and without further introduction, we will begin our presentation. Again, thank for your attention and we hope you enjoy and participate in today's presentation. See? Your time is almost over.

At this point in this book, you have almost made it to the end, or you skipped to here; it makes no difference. This means that you have a longer attention span than most executives. You are either a Zen Master executive who is only reading this book to find one gem of wisdom in these many pages (which you will know is not wisdom, but an interesting illusion), or you are less than an executive, and think this book contains the esoteric secrets of becoming one. Both paths lead to heaven! Do not give up! This last part is for those of you who feel like you'll never make it.

The Management Multiverse

The "many-worlds" interpretation of
quantum mechanics not only contradicts the
"wave-function collapse" theory, but is also
useful in management. In particular, if there is no
wavefunction to collapse when it is observed,
most managers are wasting a lot of time
worrying about appearances. Further, since the
multiverse contains an infinite number of parallel
universes or "quantum worlds," how important
could it be that you succeed in this one?

If the various universes in the multiverse
could leak into each other ... After searching for
what seemed like months, and his parentage

never truly in doubt, he was delivered, bound hand and foot, to his father's mansion. The butler stared in shock as he was unceremoniously dropped onto the Persian rug in the drawing room. His father untied his bonds and he staggered to his feet. I remember noticing, as I stood by the massive fireplace, idly toying with an iron poker, that he looked far less dangerous in profile, feeble and cerebral in fact! One moment I pitied him, and the next I felt that I would leap forward and strike him. Instead, I poked the fire and mused over the many twists of fate in one life.

Not sure what that was – probably a bit of leakage from another universe, but that can't happen, so please disregard. Since the parallel universes don't communicate, no worries about the "parallel you" getting a loser reputation in the other worlds. In fact, if you could see the other worlds, at least one of the "parallel you" is already Chairman of the Board. On the other hand, one of them is in jail, so leave those worlds alone, for now. Since the "you" who is reading this book feels that the career climb is moving too slow, I am going to open the obscure secrets of the Weightless Float to the Top, in the next chapter.

…This was perhaps the darkest moment of his life. He would later write to his lifelong friend and confidant, "I had no more strength, no love nor anger; my world had not come to an end – it had come to terrifying life!"

There it goes again … this is troubling... we will have it checked.

The Four Unspeakable Truths
of the Weightless Float to the Top

1. As you have suspected all along, everyone in your workplace is insane, only desperately clinging to their role to keep from being institutionalized. There is no "sane" person.

2. In fact, people are not real.

3. There is no difference between communication that makes sense, and random word combinations.

4. There is no businesslike demeanor, no etiquette, no best practice, no profit and no loss.

Actors portraying megalomaniac, paranoid, delusional businesspeople could hold successful meetings at the biggest and best companies with no preparation! What does that tell you? It is time for you to find new, "ways to be."

Remember, "I never said "ma petite Babette" - which would be redundant anyway. (However, if you are reading this my little Babette, do not forget me)."

Also remember: The power of a manager is in inverse proportion to his attempts to add value. This is only logical; consider a manager who finds an opportunity to add value: The manager is giddy with excitement, "Finally something I remember how to do!" He comes to every meeting, reviews every document, corrects everyone's misstatements, and will not let anyone finish a sentence. He could just send a letter to the Board of Directors stating, "I am insecure in my position, underserving of my rank, and unable to add strategic value, therefore I am wallowing in the tactical with people who are paid much less to do the same thing." Does this mean that you should do nothing all day? Yes, it does - have I not made that clear yet?

So you have reached the end of this tiny book. For those self-indulgent characters who read the end at the beginning, you did not read this book yet, so you are not a better manager – sorry. For those who read the book in its entirety, your attention span is too long – you may not make it in management. Again, we are sorry. (This is too much bad news, let's try something else). Congratulations on your purchase of this book! Excellent use of your time and money! You are now a master manager! Go and do!